Human Generativity

Volume IV: The New 3Rs:
Relating, Representing, and Reasoning

Robert R. Carkhuff, Ph.D.

Donald M. Benoit, M.Ed.

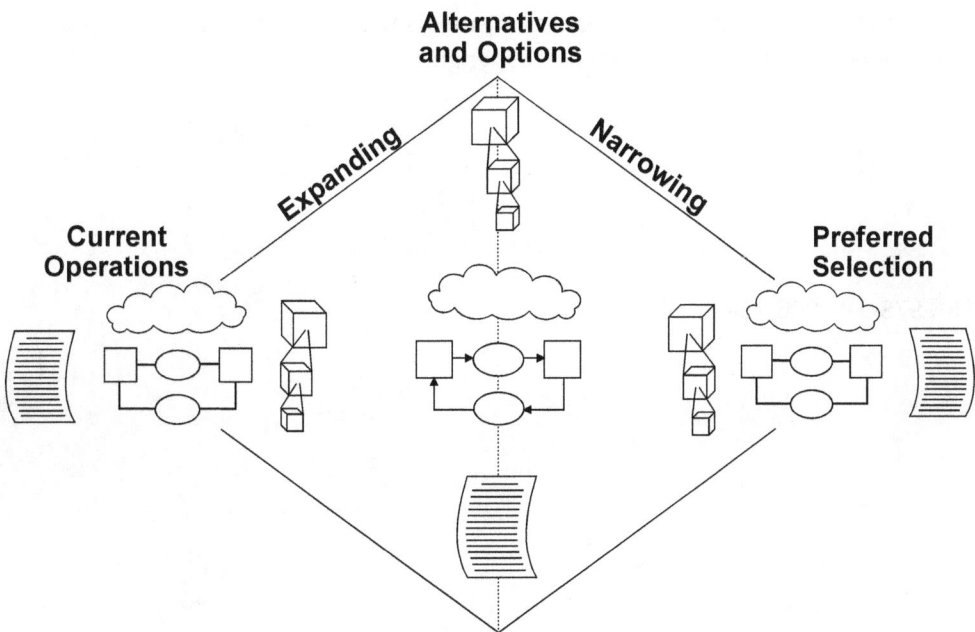

Alternatives and Options

Expanding

Narrowing

Current Operations

Preferred Selection

Generativity Thinking System

Published by: HRD Press, Inc.
                 22 Amherst Road
                 Amherst, MA 01002
                 800-822-2801 (U.S. and Canada)
                 413-253-3488
                 413-253-3490 (fax)

ISBN 978-1-59996-158-3

Editorial services by Robert W. Carkhuff
Production services by Jean S. Miller
Cover design by Eileen Klockars
Promotion by Swift Global Media

Human Generativity
Volume IV: The New 3Rs:
Relating, Representing, and Reasoning

Contents

About the Authors

Among the most-cited scientists of the 20th century and already the most prolific in the 21st century, Robert R. Carkhuff is Chairman of **The McLean Project** and the author of *The Human Sciences.*

Donald M. Benoit is Director, Curriculum Development, **Carkhuff Thinking Systems, Inc.,** a corporation dedicated to generative thinking and organizational architecture.

Their full body of work may be viewed on the websites:

www.mcleanproject.com

www.carkhuffgenerativitylibrary.com

Carkhuff boldly confronts our current socioeconomic crises:

"Generativity is the solution!"

"What is the question?"

Preface

What is this book about?

Welcome! This is a book about thinking skills. It is meant to help us become more creative, more innovative, more generative and more skilled thinkers. It is also a book about freedom. The ability and opportunity to create a new response defines freedom. If we tend to follow others and don't direct our energies to generating our own new ideas, then we are missing opportunities to use our freedom. To actualize our freedom we need to think creatively—innovatively—generatively!

In *The New 3Rs: Relating, Representing, and Reasoning*, skills for freedom and thinking are demystified.

Here is what you will find in this book:

- **Chapter 1** builds a systems view of individual freedom.

- **Chapter 2** introduces critical skills for thinking and individual freedom— The New 3Rs: Relating, Representing and Reasoning.

- **Chapter 3** presents the skills of *relating* to information and the people who produce it. It explains the behavioral steps involved in getting, giving and merging with people and other sources of information.

- **Chapter 4** explains three useful ways for *representing* information. We are introduced to cognitive structures for building sentences, systems and schematic models.

- **Chapter 5** guides us through a *reasoning* process for creating information. We are introduced to systematic methods for exploring, understanding and acting upon information to generate new and better information.

- **Chapter 6** summarizes the skills of *The New 3Rs* and challenges us to unleash our thinking, enable our freedom, and empower a generation of free people—"The Possibilities People."

Why would teachers want to read this book?

We are each unique. The combination of the natural physical wiring of each brain and the connections nurtured by the interaction of each brain with the environmental stimuli of life experiences makes us each unique, each special, each gifted in our own way.

It does not matter which age group, which grade, or which academic subjects we have been hired to teach, we are all challenged with the goal of nurturing the growth of a room full of unique people. It surely is a complex opportunity, and a great responsibility. Teaching requires much of our own creativity to truly empower each learner with what they want and need.

How can skills found in *The New 3Rs* help? The skills will help you to relate with each of your learners; the skills will help you to demystify the information that you have been hired to impart; the skills will give you a method to guide you as you work with your learners to reason—to create hypotheses to test. Most importantly, once you teach your learners these same skills, they will become your thinking partners. They, too, will become empowered and freed to perform, learn, and create.

Why would parents want to read this book?

As parents, we are our children's first teachers. We are also enduring figures in each other's lives. They are a part of us, and we of them. Family experiences involve mutual growth and development. Family life is a great opportunity, privilege, and responsibility. Parenting is a creative endeavor, too, and we will-ingly and lovingly take on the challenge. How can we best parent our children, the neighborhood kids, and the children of our community?

The skills of *The New 3Rs* can help us parent. We will learn to better relate with our children by expanding our interpersonal communication skills. We will learn to better represent information—to help our children demystify how the world works. Parenting is an opportunity for us to expand our own understanding of how things work, as well. We will become aware of some new behaviors that we can use when called upon to reason—to solve problems and create opportunities. Most enjoyably, it is a great satisfaction to witness our children using their unique minds to solve their own problems and create their own opportunities.

Why would learners want to read this book?

Most any learner can learn about thinking skills from this book. If you find too many words that you are not familiar with, then just look at the graphics. Try sitting with someone else—a friend, parent, or teacher—and discuss the graphics. Maybe the other person has read the words in this book and can share some of what they read. If you are comfortable with the words in this text, go for it, and read it too!

The New 3Rs can help young people relate better with everybody. That means a better line of communication with friends, parents, teachers, coaches, neighbors, and better communication with potential employers. You can learn to organize information and represent it more clearly. After learning "information represent-ing skills" your homework will not be as confusing or overwhelming. You will get better grades. Once you learn more about reasoning skills you will be more skilled about understanding what is expected of you by others, and what you really want to do. You will have some new ways to analyze information and situations, and have some new methods for making your own good decisions. You will know how to make a plan, complete it, and decide what worked and what didn't.

Why would workers want to read this book?

The economy has elevated its requirements of us. People with higher-paying jobs are often paid well because they are being asked to think. They are also being asked to learn new technologies and then use them to solve problems, lots of problems. So, to earn more per hour, per day, and per year, we need to become better learners and better thinkers!

The New 3Rs can help you get a job if you don't have one, help you in your current job, or prepare you for an even better one. Did you know that a majority of work-related problems are due to communication issues? You can learn to be a more skilled communicator when relating with managers, supervisors, co-workers, and customers. Information representing skills help you clarify what you read and organize what you say or write. Reasoning skills help you clarify your goals so you can achieve them, and start you thinking about anything and everything. There is so much to learn and so much to create. You, too, are unique and looking for ways to develop and apply your uniqueness. You can get paid for using your creativity—your ability to think!

Why would managers and executives want to read this book?

You are responsible for your work unit, or maybe even for a whole organization. You don't need any convincing as to your requirements for thinking, problem solving, and the creation of opportunities. You live with these requirements!

The New 3Rs can help you and your employees. Relating skills empower communication. Representing skills enable one to organize complex information into easily understandable, connected parts. Then, there is "reasoning" that is required of you: goal-setting, problem and opportunity analyses, expanding to generate new ideas and new options, decision-making, programmatic planning, leading the performance of projects, and the evaluation of performance. This is what is expected of every manager and executive. These skills are for you and for the people who work with you.

Let's empower you, "put-power-in-you." Your students, your children, your friends and families, your teachers and classmates, your future employers and employees, and your communities are looking forward to all the many important, creative contributions you will make during your lifetime! We invite you to develop the generative, creative thinker that is you! Begin with this book—*The New 3Rs: Relating, Representing, and Reasoning.*

RRC
DMB

June, 2013
McLean, Virginia

I

Introduction

1
Freedom—A Systems View

What Is Freedom?

What is "freedom"? Every dictionary definition of freedom includes the words "absence of constraint." What are these constraints? If we are free, what are we free from? If we are free, what is it that we have? We need to know what is present when we are free; otherwise, we will not know when we have lost our freedom.

Let's take a systems view of freedom. A systems view of freedom will help us begin to determine how free we are and what we can do to enable and empower our own individual freedom and the freedom of others. Within this systems view we will find ourselves and our levels of freedom.

A Systems View of Freedom

For a moment, consider the commonalities of all systems. Our systems view has five parts: the conditions or context within which the rest of the system operates; the inputs or resources that the system uses; the processes or activities that change the inputs; the outputs or results of the processes; and feedback information that can tell about the quantity or quality of each of the parts of the system.

A graphic of a system is presented on the next page. In the pages that follow, we will visit each of the five parts of a system to help us better understand freedom.

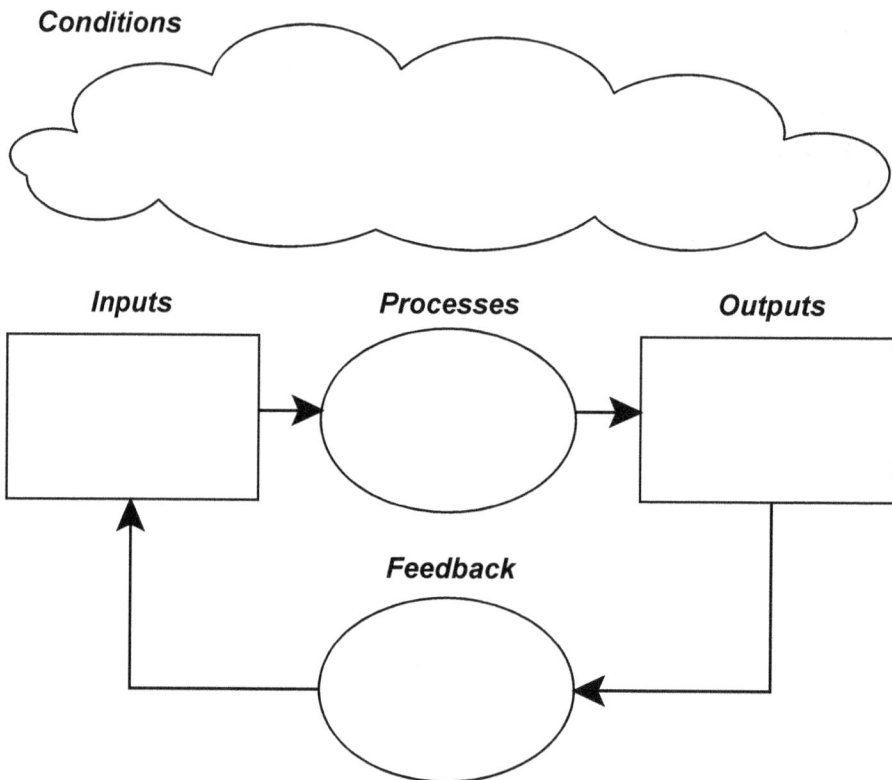

Conditions

Inputs   **Processes**   **Outputs**

Feedback

The Conditions for Individual Freedom

Sometimes we feel surrounded, because we are. We are surrounded by the conditions or context within which we live, learn and work.

Conditions are powerful. We are humbled by the strength of the conditions about us. Conditions are processes that impact us and cannot be impacted or changed by us.

Conditions either support our freedom or constrain it. Do we have the humility to recognize and accept the conditions we cannot change?

Do we see our personal health, our job opportunities, our schools, and the safety of our neighborhoods, for example, as conditions that we must accept or as things we can impact or change? Do we have the willingness and the skills to change the conditions of our lives? If we do, then we refuse to accept our current constraints. Instead, we will take "conditions" and treat them as inputs to our system, inputs that we believe we can act on and change.

Certainly, we live within the constraints of some conditions that we cannot change. Yet, we will find our individual freedom in what we "do" to change our conditions through the power of our initiatives.

Conditions

...powers that impact us that we do not believe we can change.

The Inputs to Individual Freedom

Resource inputs include information, people, and things that impact our individual freedom.

Resource inputs are anything or anyone that we are living, learning, or working with. Inputs include all of our experiences to this point in our lives—like child-rearing, schooling, jobs, and other developmental experiences. Inputs include the food we eat and the paychecks we earn.

There are many inputs that impact our individual freedom. Sometimes we work hard to gather inputs that will enable us to live free. At other times, inputs arrive without an expressed request for them. It is what we **DO** with these resources that will determine our levels of freedom.

Conditions

...powers that impact us that we do not believe we can change.

Inputs

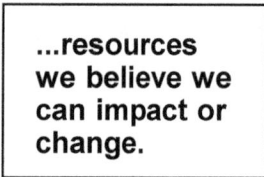

...resources we believe we can impact or change.

The Processes of Individual Freedom

The processes of individual freedom are our actions. Processes are anything we "do." For example, they may include how we approach tasks at school, how we work, how we get along with others, how we take a stand for what is important to us, and how we solve problems. Processes are about taking inputs and doing something with them. Processes are the actions we take to change resource inputs into something of our choosing.

It is our actions that determine whether we live free or not. This book is all about learning effective behaviors to enable our actions—our freedom. This book is about skills to empower freedom. This book is about what we can **DO** to become free. This book is about what free people "do."

We are defined by what we do. Our freedom is defined by what we choose to do.

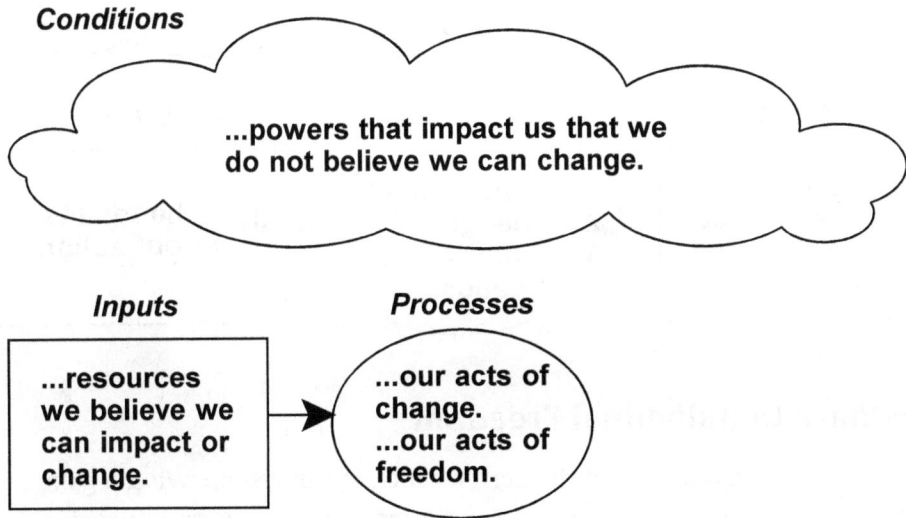

Conditions

...powers that impact us that we
do not believe we can change.

Inputs

...resources
we believe we
can impact or
change.

Processes

...our acts of
change.
...our acts of
freedom.

The Outputs of Individual Freedom

Outputs are the results of our actions. Outputs are what happens when we act. Outputs include results for others as well as for ourselves. As parents or teachers, the development of our children and learners is a result of our child-rearing and teaching processes. As workers, the products we make and the services we deliver are the outputs of our work. As learners, the projects we complete are outputs of our learning processes. Outputs are what happens when we act on our choices. Outputs are what results when we act on our freedom.

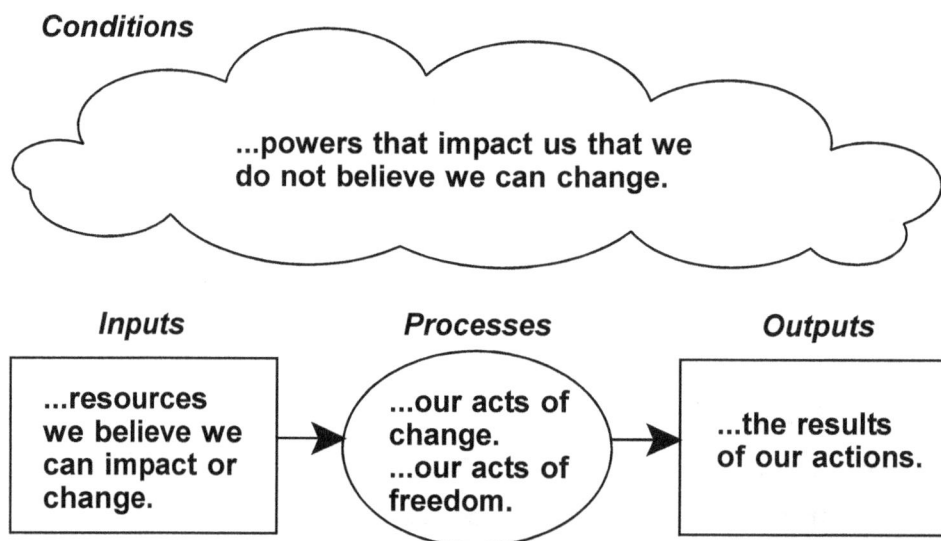

Conditions

...powers that impact us that we
do not believe we can change.

Inputs	**Processes**	**Outputs**
...resources we believe we can impact or change.	...our acts of change. ...our acts of freedom.	...the results of our actions.

Feedback to Individual Freedom

Feedback is information about the performance of our system. We can gain feedback about any part of a system: conditions, outputs, inputs, or processes. Let's take a look at how we can measure each part of our systems diagram of individual freedom.

Feedback about our individual freedom involves measuring qualities and quantities of the conditions or contexts we live in. Do they enable or hinder our actions? Do we choose to re-categorize some of these conditions as inputs and then go on to change them?

Feedback about our individual freedom involves measuring the results or outputs of our actions. What did we produce today? How have we marked our presence—to show that we have lived?

Feedback about our individual freedom involves measuring how we use our resources or inputs. Do we produce more than we consume? Do we give more than we receive, or do we take more than we deserve?

Feedback about our individual freedom involves measuring our processes or how we live—freely or not. This book will present suggested behaviors or actions to help us live free.

It has been often said, "We get what we measure." So, if we want to live free, then we need to have a way to measure individual freedom.

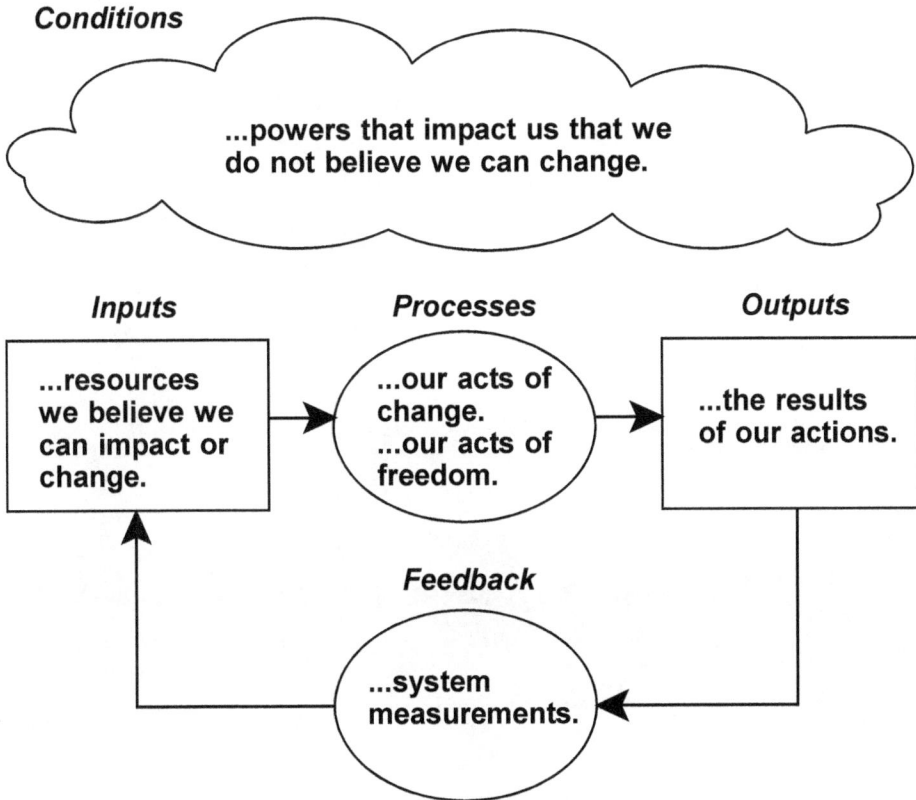

Conditions

...powers that impact us that we do not believe we can change.

Inputs

...resources we believe we can impact or change.

Processes

...our acts of change.
...our acts of freedom.

Outputs

...the results of our actions.

Feedback

...system measurements.

A Systems View of Freedom

Summary

By considering each of the parts of the systems in which we live, we are beginning to think about what makes us free or not free.

- Conditions are the powers that impact upon us that we do not believe we can change.

- Inputs are the resources we believe we can impact or change.

- Processes are our acts of change—our acts of freedom.

- Outputs are the results of our actions.

- Feedback is information about the qualities and quantity of our system ingredients.

It is helpful to take a systems view of freedom. We better understand our freedom when we measure the outputs or results of our actions, the inputs or resources we use, and the context or conditions within which we live. Most importantly, a systems view of freedom helps us to focus on the simple fact that our own actions, our own activities, and our own processes for living define our freedom. We must take responsibility for our own freedom. Simply stated, people are free when they act freely.

Our freedom is defined by our processes, our actions. We are what we do, not what we dream about doing or talk about doing. What is preventing us from actualizing our freedom? What are the processes, activities, or actions of free people? How can we be free?

2

Possibilities Thinking and Individual Freedom

Freedom Requires "Change"

We may experience a variety of constraints upon our freedom. Some of us may live within a culture or state that places limitations on our travel, a limitation on free speech, or a limitation on the right to assemble with others. If we live in an unsafe neighborhood, then our physical freedoms are also limited. Physical constraints may involve insufficient food or inadequate shelter or health care. We may feel constrained by a lack of opportunities for employment or advancement. What will we do about these constraints?

If we accept these constraints or limitations as conditions—powers that impact us that we do not believe we can change—then we will remain constrained and unfree.

Freedom from constraints requires action. Someone has to initiate change. In some instances, many people may be needed to join together to initiate change. It is what we "do" to initiate change that sets us free. It is inertia, a lack of change, that is the ultimate constraint upon our freedom. Without movement and change, without a "new behavior," we are shackled to an unchanging future—a future without freedom.

Levels of Thinking and Levels of Freedom

What is it that free people do? Free people are agents of change. Free people are thinking people. Thinking is the source of willful, human initiative. Thinking is what makes people free. This is the premise of this book. It is the premise of our lives. Ultimately, it is the quality of our thinking that determines our level of freedom to initiate change.

There are different approaches to thinking and living free. We call these approaches generative thinking, discriminative learning, and conditioned responding.

Generative Thinking means creating a new response or product. **Discriminative Learning** means finding and selecting a response or product that someone else has created. **Conditioned Responding** means performing a habitual behavior that we have been conditioned by reinforcers to make.

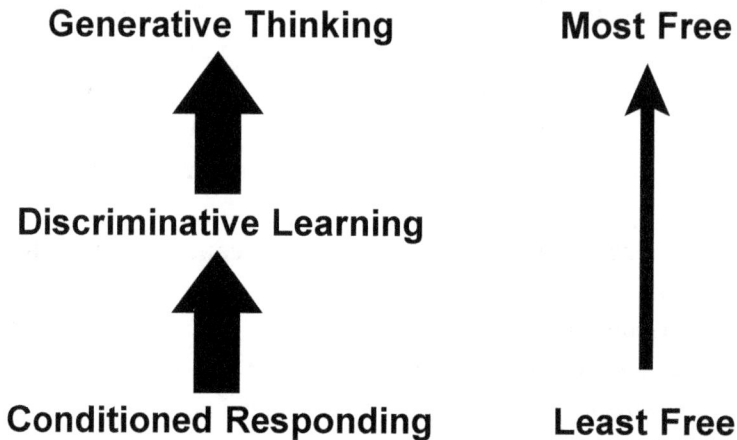

Generative Thinking ↑ Most Free ↑

Discriminative Learning ↑

Conditioned Responding Least Free

The Conditioned Responder

When we are **Conditioned Responders,** we are the least free. When faced with a problem, we simply emit the response we were conditioned to make.

Can conditioned responses be useful? Absolutely. These are our reflex responses. We use them when we react instinctively to dangers or perform reactively to stimuli.

Habits are another term for conditioned responses. Good habits serve us well, while bad habits continue to serve us poorly. When does a good habit become a bad one? When it no longer helps us to grow.

When we are Conditioned Responders, there are no options or degrees of freedom for us. There is only the one acceptable response that we have been conditioned to make. Each time we act habitually, without thinking, we are missing an opportunity to be free.

How else can we respond to be more free? We may increase choices by finding a better response, one that someone else has already created (discriminative learning). Or, we may gain still greater freedom by using our own brainpower to generate or create a new response (generative thinking).

The Discriminative Learner

When we are **Discriminative Learners,** we are much more free than when we are Conditioned Responders. Yet, we are still much less free than when we are Generative Thinkers. As Discriminative Learners, when faced with a problem, we search from among known responses for one that we believe will work best. Then, we apply the response.

As Discriminative Learners we use a process that involves learning and discriminating. As dedicated learners, we want to know what other people have done when faced with a similar situation. As dedicated learners, we love to read, we search the Internet for answers, and we ask others for advice. Then, from the assembled collection of information, we select or "discriminate" what to do.

Discriminative learning is an infinitely more powerful way to use our brainpower than conditioned responding. As Discriminative Learners, we can potentially take advantage of the history of all people. As Discriminative Learners, our choices or degrees of freedom are measured by our abilities to access and learn from others, and then choose a wise and useful course. Discriminative learning can serve us well, because learning is an efficient process for gaining options and choices.

Discriminative learning, however, is not always effective, and may even be harmful. When the responses that we "find" are no longer adequate, when they don't work, when they are not accurate, they no longer help us to grow.

If we only look to others for answers, then we will never unleash our own generative thinking powers and, so, never actualize our own freedom.

The Generative Thinker

When we are **Generative Thinkers,** we go beyond known responses to create new ones. We are most free when we generate new responses, new ideas, and new solutions.

There have been many great scientists and artists throughout history who, in select parts of their lives, have actualized their creativity. We see it in the products they have left behind for us. Can we become creative and generative thinkers too? Can we actualize our freedom?

To become Generative Thinkers we must first free ourselves of our utter reliance on habits (conditioned responding), and then free ourselves from only looking to others for answers (discriminative learning). Where they serve us well, we will build upon these responses, but we must willingly and intentionally go beyond these two approaches.

The purpose of this book is to introduce readers to **Generative Thinking.** The pages that follow will present skills for generative thinking. These "thinking skills" are a series of behaviors that we can use to help us to create new responses and solutions to problems and opportunities we may face. These are not "lock-step behaviors," they are "interactive behaviors." They are not "limiting behaviors," they are provided to stimulate our own thinking about how we can become more creative, more generative, more free.

We call these possibilities thinking skills **The New 3Rs—Relating, Representing and Reasoning.**

The New 3Rs of Possibilities Thinking and Individual Freedom

Actualizing Individual Freedom by Relating

All generative thinking begins with **Relating.** This book will introduce us to the skills of relating: *getting, giving,* and *merging* with information. We will learn to **get** information effectively—to become *empathic.* We will learn to **give** information effectively—to become *additive.* We will learn to **merge** with information—to become *inclusive* of others and their points of view.

RELATING

Merge
Give
Get

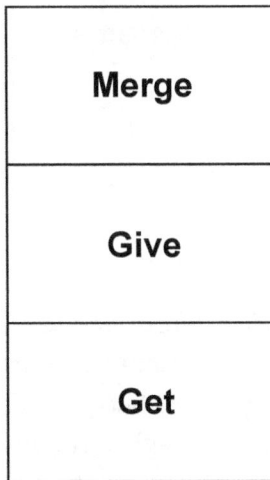

No scientist or artist has ever had a generative or creative breakthrough without relating with, connecting with, the information about his or her area of interest.

The process of relating with people and with other sources of information connects us to an unfolding of variability and variance (differences). Relating connects us to rich sources of information to stimulate our creativity. Without "relating," we are limited to our own perspectives.

The skills of relating by getting, giving, and merging will help anyone connect with others and with information. In concert with additional thinking skills, skilled relating behaviors will help us create solutions to problems and connect with additional opportunities for change.

Relating behaviors enable individual freedom.

Actualizing Individual Freedom by Representing

All generative thinking requires the **Representing,** or the representation, of information. This book will introduce us to skills for representing information with *sentences, systems,* and *schematics.*

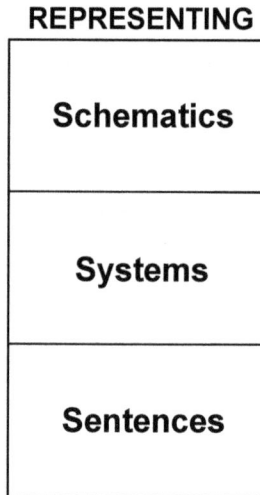

REPRESENTING

Schematics
Systems
Sentences

We will learn to improve our use of words and **sentences** and become *articulate reporters.* We will learn to develop **systems** diagrams to become *systems scientists.* We will learn to use **schematics** to become *information modelers.*

All scientists and artists work through iterations of representations of their ideas. Scientific discovery and artistic creativity culminate in information products—a formula, a protocol, a design for a product, a poem, a book, a song, a painting, a sculpture.

We, too, work through our own creativity by producing iterations of representations of our ideas. Ultimately, we culminate our own creativity in information products: a new method for accomplishing something, a new verbal or written response, a new artistic product.

Although each field of knowledge has its own historical terms and methods of information representation, the language and skills for representing information with sentences, systems, and schematics can serve to increase the creativity of anyone.

The effective representation of information enables individual freedom.

Actualizing Individual Freedom by Reasoning

All generative thinking involves **Reasoning,** processes that can result in creating new ideas—new information. The pages of this book will introduce us to skills for reasoning: *exploring, understanding,* and *acting.*

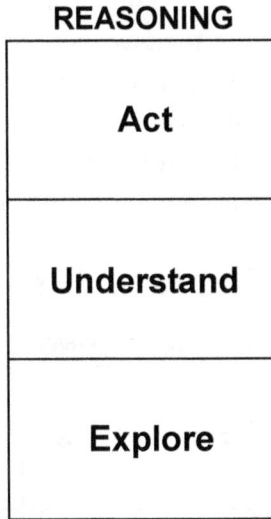

REASONING

Act
Understand
Explore

We will begin to explore problems and opportunities by setting goals and analyzing information. We will learn to expand this information and become more effective *explorers.* We will learn to understand how to better solve problems and create opportunities by narrowing purposefully to become *innovators.* We will learn to act upon our creative ideas by planning, performing, and evaluating as *hypothesis testers.*

Creativity and problem-solving involve *change.* But what do we want or need to change? How can we determine what we currently have so we can better consider possibilities for change? Are we missing some important ingredient or process for change? Is there a "gap" between what we have and what we believe we need or want? How do we go beyond current known options? How do we decide what changes we think might work? How do we effectively test our hypotheses for change? These are all questions we ask of ourselves as we *reason.*

The reasoning skills behaviors described in this book for exploring, understanding, and acting can be applied to help anyone create change.

Effective reasoning, ultimately, defines individual freedom.

Possibilities Thinking and Individual Freedom

Good habits serve us well, while bad habits continue to serve us poorly. Each time we act habitually, without thinking, we are missing an opportunity to be free.

Learning is an efficient process for gaining options and choices; however, if we only look to others for answers, then we will never unleash our own generative thinking powers and, so, never actualize our own freedom.

Thinking is what makes people free.

The New 3Rs: Relating, Representing and Reasoning are skills that enable us to actualize possibilities thinking and individual freedom.

The New 3Rs

RELATING	REPRESENTING	REASONING
Merge	Schematics	Act
Give	Systems	Understand
Get	Sentences	Explore

II

The New 3Rs

3
R¹—Relating

Getting, Giving, and Merging

All thinking begins with relating. Relating means connecting. Thinking requires connecting with others and with information. The skills of relating can be described as *getting, giving,* and *merging* with others and with information. Research tells us that we are probably not as skilled at relating as we might initially think we are. We can all benefit from improving our relating skills.

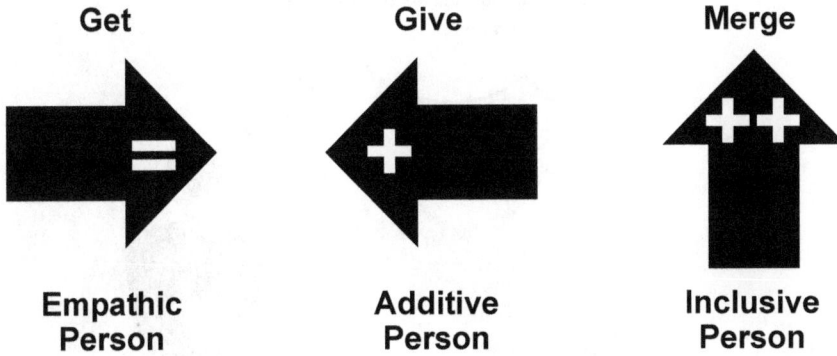

Get	Give	Merge
⟹ =	+ ⟸	⬆ ++
Empathic Person	**Additive Person**	**Inclusive Person**

"Getting" Skills

We relate by *"getting."* Getting information means acquiring some message that has meaning. While the information has meaning for its authors, we relate to find out what this message is saying and to learn why it is meaningful for its authors. What are the skills we use for getting information?

Get = ⟹

Getting by Attending, Observing, Listening, and Responding

We acquire information by paying attention, observing, listening, and responding. How would we describe the specific behaviors for each of these four skills? Let's see how our own descriptions match up against the skill descriptions that follow.

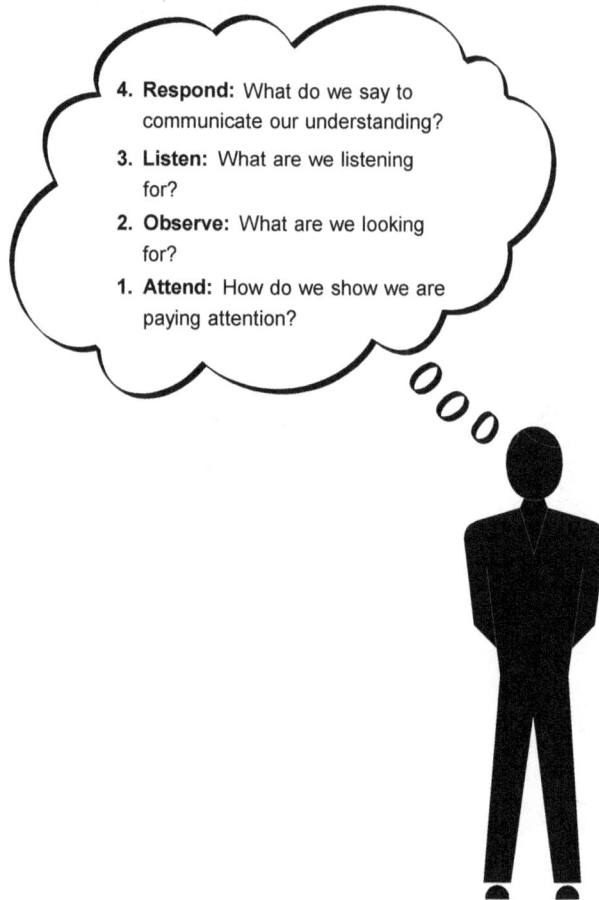

4. **Respond:** What do we say to communicate our understanding?

3. **Listen:** What are we listening for?

2. **Observe:** What are we looking for?

1. **Attend:** How do we show we are paying attention?

Getting by Attending

We feel welcomed when others pay attention to us. They prepare the context for us and are ready to be with us. They face us, or square themselves to us, and lean toward us. They make eye contact. When others fail to prepare a context for us, fail to face us, or fail to look at us, we feel neglected or even rejected. We feel disconnected from them and feel that we are not important to them. Getting information from people or from other information sources starts with paying attention.

- **Prepare**

- **Square and lean**

- **Make eye contact**

Attending to Others

Attending to Information

Getting by Observing

Observing means focusing our eyes and our minds upon what we see before us. One way to focus our observations is to look for appearance and behaviors. Observing appearance means looking for specific characteristics so we can identify the distinctiveness in what or who we are seeing. Observing behavior means looking at activity, movement, or change. When we observe human behavior, we are seeing how a person acts or reacts to changing situations.

- **Observe appearance**

- **Observe behaviors**

- **Consider inferences**

Observing Others   **Observing Information**

Once we have collected information from our observations of appearance and behavior, we may find that we have noticed enough information so we can make an initial inference or hypothesis about what we see. Often, we will want to gather still more information before we consider using our initial inferences as a basis for any initiatives with the other person.

When we observe others, we can learn a lot if we look for distinctive features, initiative, or reactive behaviors upon which we may formulate a tentative inference or hypothesis about what we observe.

Getting by Listening

When we listen, we hear details. We hear sentences, word-for-word. We hear music, note-for-note. If the details seem important enough, we try to remember them.

When we are successful at listening for details, we can repeat the words or sing the tune. Sometimes we don't try to remember all the details. Instead, we listen for themes. Listening for themes means listening to identify a unifying or central topic or subject. When we listen, we listen for a reason: to collect specifics or to discover a theme.

- **Resist distractions**

- **Listen for specifics**

- **Discover the theme**

Listening to Others

Listening to Information

Sometimes we miss things because we get interference from external distractions. Sometimes we get interference from internal distractions, like focusing upon our own ideas. Sometimes we get caught up in all the details of what we are hearing and miss the theme. We could all be better listeners.

Getting by Responding Interchangeably

Next, we need to find out if we accurately understood what was communicated to us. We verify our understanding by formulating and offering interchangeable responses to content, feeling, or meaning. People give us the facts or content in their message. They also communicate their feelings or emotions. Which emotion they express and how strongly they express it is important for us to find out.

3. Interchangeable Meaning

> You're (feeling) because (reason) .

2. Interchangeable Feeling

> You're (feeling) .

1. Interchangeable Content

> You're saying (content) .

When we communicate an accurate interchangeable response, our communication is experienced by the originators of the information as equal to what they intended to communicate to us: *"Yes, that's it. That's what I meant!"* People will tell us if we are on target or not. Responding interchangeably is a powerful tool for connecting with people. People don't really know if we are hearing or seeing what they are communicating to us until we acknowledge what they are telling and showing us.

Sometimes we relate directly with information and are not able to check our understanding with its authors. In those cases, we may share our interchangeable responses with other people we know who have also read or heard the same information. In this way, we can check the accuracy of our understanding, even if we do not have direct access to the author of the information. When we share our interchangeable responses with others, we can test our understanding of what was said. We can find out what others think was said and see if it matches with our understanding.

Summarizing Getting

Sometimes we fail to pay full attention. If we don't prepare for people or other sources of information, face them, or give them eye contact, they may feel alienated or rejected.

We can gather important information if we are vigilant of the appearance and behaviors of the information or its sources; only then can we make inferences or hypotheses about what we are seeing.

Often, when we fail to listen, it is because we have succumbed to distractions. We may be distracted because we are too intensely focused upon our own thoughts and leave no room for other information.

Interchangeable responding gives us a chance to find out if we have understood the information that was communicated to us. Sometimes we can offer our responses directly to the person who is giving it to us. Sometimes we measure our responsiveness by telling or showing our interchangeable statements with others who have heard and seen the same message.

Getting means attending, observing, listening, and responding interchangeably.

4.	**Responding Interchangeably**	• Say, "You're _(feeling)_ because _(reason)_ ." • Say, "You're _(feeling)_ ." • Say, "You're saying _(content)_ ."
3.	**Listening**	• Discover the theme • Listen for specifics • Resist distractions
2.	**Observing**	• Consider inferences • Observe behaviors • Observe appearance
1.	**Attending**	• Make eye contact • Square and lean • Prepare

The Benefits of Getting

Interchangeable responding is the culminating behavior of the skills for getting information. In studies of tens of thousands of people, we have found that some naturally respond to others with expressions that are interchangeable to the *content* they hear and see. Still, fewer respond interchangeably to the *feelings* that others express. Without training in, or exposure to modeling of, the formulation of interchangeable responses to meaning—the feeling and reasons that others are expressing—it is a rare event for people to respond to others in this way. Yet, research clearly tells us that getting information by responding interchangeably to content, feeling, and meaning is powerfully effective. When people formulate interchangeable responses to content, feeling, and meaning, we say they are "empathic." This means that they are "in tune" with the message and the messenger and match what they hear and see. Everyone benefits from the skilled responsiveness of *The Empathic Person.*

THE EMPATHIC PERSON

"Giving" Skills

We also relate by "giving." When we give information, we organize it and deliver it so others will understand it. We begin by organizing information for ourselves, to clarify what it is and what it means for us. If we intend to share information with others, we will need to organize it so they will understand it, too. We deliver information that is important to us because we believe that others will find our message meaningful to them as well. What are the skills of giving information?

Giving by Initiating Additively

We communicate information by doing, showing, and telling. We *do* by modeling performance. We *show* with a variety of visual tools. We *tell* with words and sounds.

Across the world, talking is the primary method of information dissemination. Would others benefit from more visual representations of what we are trying to communicate to them? If we have a physical performance that we would like others to experience and understand, then we can model these behaviors to best deliver our message.

Giving by Doing

Giving by doing means physically modeling specific behaviors. Most tasks are not purely intellectual ones, where the only physical movements that take place are within our brains. Most tasks include other physical performances: we write, we draw, we apply physical forces, we sing, we play a musical instrument, we build a physical product. In short, we *do*.

We model performance when we would like others to better understand our own performance, or because we would like others to imitate our performance. To model performance requires that we first define our own behaviors. The more that we can get others to translate what we are modeling into specific physical behaviors, the easier it will be to involve them and give them new skills and behaviors.

When we communicate by modeling performance, we establish a basis for comparison so others will be better able to judge the qualities of their own performances.

Giving by Showing

How many times have we heard that a picture is worth a thousand words? Imagine the value of a "good picture," a "great chart," or a "useful map." How many words are they worth?

Showing demonstrates what something looks like and how it works. We can give information, for example, by showing pictures, graphics, maps, and charts. We can use TV and video and direct others to web sites. How well information is represented is essential to how much lasting impact it can make on others. Showing is an important and useful way to disseminate information.

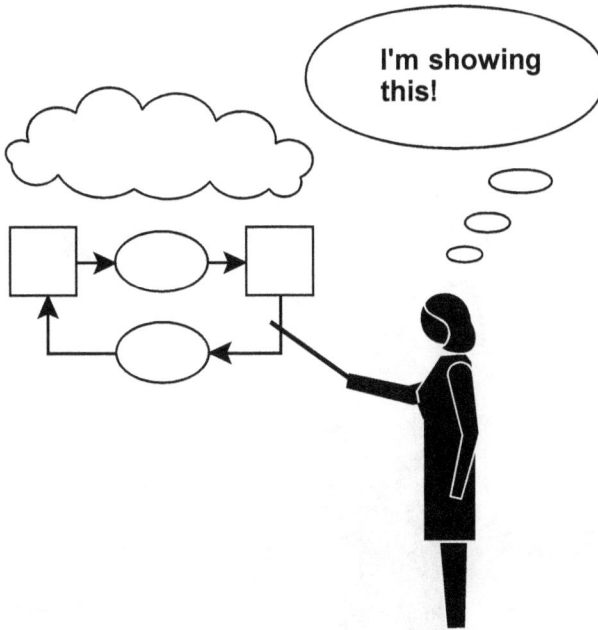

Giving by Telling

Great storytellers bring us along with them on a journey. We never leave our seats. They do it all with words. They help us build images with visual descriptions. Sometimes they change voices to present different characters. Their stories have movement, their descriptions bring us from place to place and from event to event. Then, the story ends with an image or sound for us to hold onto. We have much that we can learn from great orators and storytellers.

When we give information by telling, we ask ourselves to be great storytellers. We ask even more from our intended recipients, because stories are not easy for listeners to remember. Telling is hard work for us. Listening is hard work, too.

Here is some advice about what you may want to include in a story you tell:

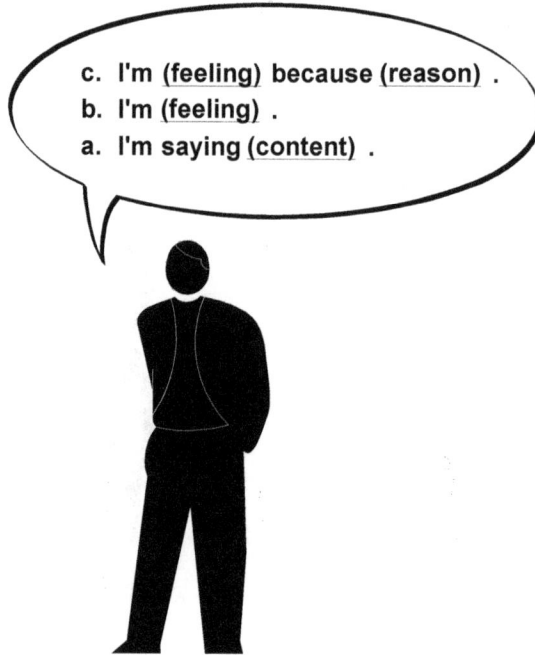

c. I'm (feeling) because (reason) .
b. I'm (feeling) .
a. I'm saying (content) .

Summarizing Giving

We can summarize the relating skills of giving information with the words *do, show* and *tell.* Doing asks performers to use their body movements or kinesthetic senses as well as their brains. Showing asks our viewers to use their eyes or visual senses as well as their brains. Telling asks our listeners to use their ears or auditory senses as well as their brains. Others benefit when we give information by all three methods: doing or demonstrating, showing or presenting, and telling or explaining.

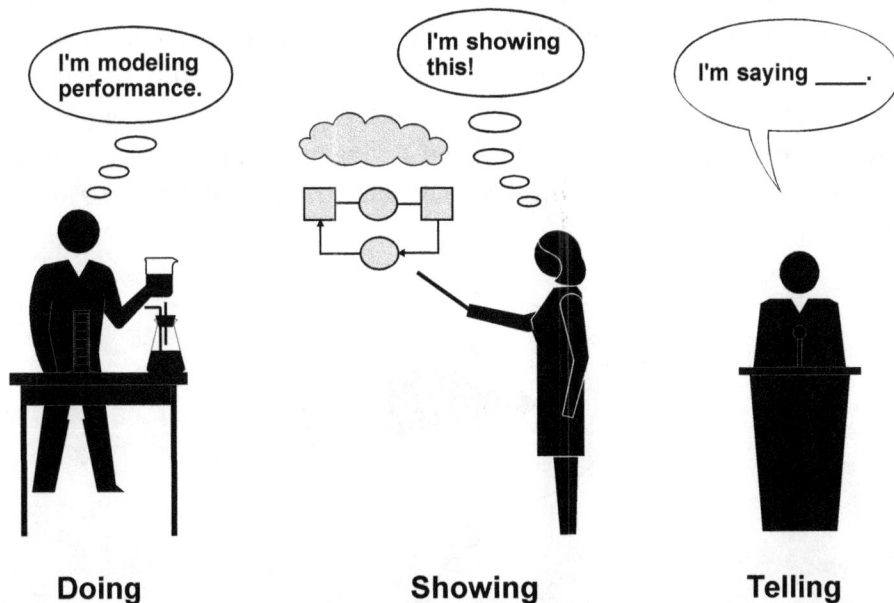

Doing **Showing** **Telling**

The Benefits of Giving

We give information to others because we have some valuable information to give. We know our content and we know our audience. We want others to come to know this content because we believe they want to know it or because we believe they need to know it. We give information to help fill a void or gap in the perspectives held by others. When we bring new information to others, we add to what they know and who they are becoming. It is a great privilege and responsibility.

Doing, showing, and telling are our methods for giving information to others. When we expand our methods for giving information to incorporate more *"doing or modeling,"* and more *"showing or presenting"* information, rather than only *"telling or explaining,"* communication improves. We increase opportunities for our message to be received and understood. Giving information plays a critical part when thinking with others. Everyone benefits from the skills of *The Additive Person.*

THE ADDITIVE PERSON

"Merging" Skills

We call the next step in relating "merging." Our use of the word *merge* does not mean that we will *"combine our identity with another person," "be absorbed"* or *"be swallowed up."* For us, *"merging"* means *"to join together, to unite"* (*Webster's Dictionary*) for a shared purpose.

The results of merging may be any of the following: "My Way," "Your Way," "Our Way," or "A New Way."

The processes of merging might involve

- **Convincing** another that "My Way" is the best way;

- **Conceding** to another that "Your Way" is the best way;

- **Negotiating** with others that "Our Way" is the preferred way; or

- **Generating** with others to create "A New Way" as the best way.

Merging means "uniting to think together."

My Way—Convincing Others

"My Way" results when other persons are convinced that my way is the best way. During the process of convincing them, others may challenge my views. They are giving me feedback about my presentation. For some reason my presentation might not connect with their experience. It either does not seem relevant (useful) or valid (accurate). If I want to try to convince them, then I will need to take some ownership for the dissonance they are experiencing. Maybe I did not organize or deliver my message adequately.

Merging to convince others involves modifying my presentation to address the issues and concerns presented by others. My modified presentations may influence their thinking. If I can convince them, then my essential message is accepted.

My Way—Convincing

Improve my presentation.

Your Way—Conceding to Others

"Your Way" is when I decide to concede my own position. When someone presents a better argument or explanation, then it is only right that I concede to a better idea.

False pride is a stubbornness and unwillingness to concede, even in the face of a better idea. We must remain humble and give other people, and their ideas, honest consideration. After all, we are often 50th percentile performers (or less) in areas that are not our areas of expertise. We have much to learn here. Even if we are 99th percentile performers in our areas of expertise, there still remains more to learn. Without humility, and a willingness to concede, we place a cap on our development. With humility, we will be able to concede to a better idea. With humility, we can continue to grow.

Here are some special situations. Sometimes we may decide to concede for reasons other than aligning with a better idea. For example, we may determine that what we disagree about is not worth the energy it will take to continue negotiating; it's not that important to us. In this instance, we may decide to concede. Alternatively, we may decide to concede because we want the other person to experience a "win." For example, adults sometimes do this when they help children win at a new game, to keep them motivated as they learn how to play.

Learning and thinking requires concession to a better idea.

Your Way—Conceding

> **Accept the other person's position.**

Our Way—Acknowledging, Negotiating, and Summarizing

What do we do if we find that we are neither convincing to others nor convinced by others? We may decide to negotiate an agreement based on our "common ground" or elevate our merging processes to generate something new, together.

"Our Way" involves both sides giving and taking to construct a position that is part "My Way" and part "Your Way." "Our Way" is all about negotiating.

We negotiate with others when we acknowledge similarities, negotiate differences, and then summarize the negotiated agreement. Acknowledging similarities means showing and telling where our messages match. Negotiating differences is the give and take between and among people who represent differing points of view. Summarizing our negotiated agreements means we are making sure all of the participants know the results of our negotiations. We relate by merging when we come together to acknowledge our similarities and negotiate our differences.

> 3. Summarize negotiated agreement
> 2. Negotiate differences
> 1. Acknowledge agreement

Our Way—Acknowledging Agreement

We acknowledge agreement by specifying our agreement. This is similar to the skill of interchangeable responding. Instead of formulating a response that is interchangeable with the message that someone else is communicating to us, we formulate a response that is interchangeable with the similarities found in multiple points of view. We acknowledge our agreement and communicate the commonalities of our messages. With the common ground identified, we can go on to the real work of merging—negotiating our differences.

Our Way—Negotiating Differences

When we negotiate our differences, we begin by showing and telling what they are. We may modify our presentation and give it to others once again. We may get modified information from others, and it may modify our thinking.

Negotiating differences typically requires that we find higher level values or goals that we can agree upon. Then, we can revisit our differences using this elevated perspective to determine what we need to change to meet our agreed-upon values or goals.

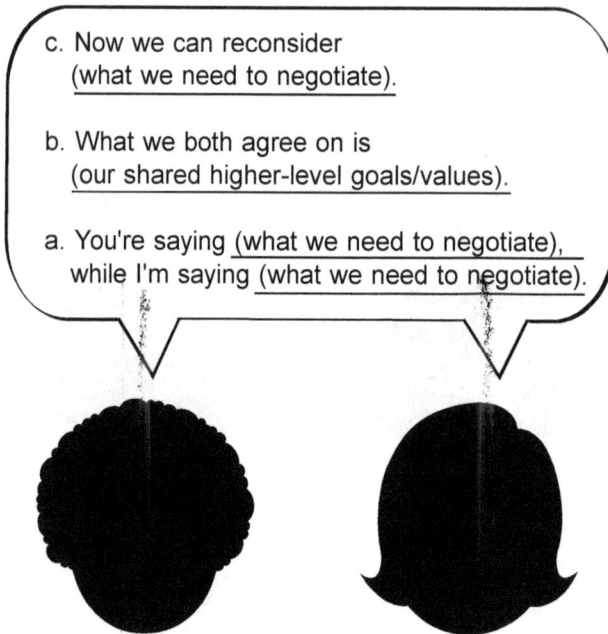

c. Now we can reconsider
   (what we need to negotiate).

b. What we both agree on is
   (our shared higher-level goals/values).

a. You're saying (what we need to negotiate),
   while I'm saying (what we need to negotiate).

Our Way—Summarizing the Negotiated Agreement

We summarize agreements and differences to reinforce others to participate in the merging experience with us. We are pleased because others are so involved and excited. We express our understanding and our excitement with others to reinforce them to merge ideas, to assemble a consolidated agreement—our agreement.

c. We're (feeling) because (reason) .

b. We're (feeling) .

a. We're saying (content) .

Our Way—Summarizing Negotiation Skills

We merge our points of view by acknowledging similarities, negotiating differences, and summarizing agreement.

Merging may not necessarily result in total agreement among parties. The process of merging, however, is a great opportunity for thinking by all of the participants.

3. Summarize negotiated agreement

c. We're (feeling) because (reason) .

b. We're (feeling) .

a. We're saying (content) .

2. Negotiate differences

c. Now we can reconsider
(what we need to negotiate).

b. What we both agree on is
(our shared higher-level goals/values).

a. You're saying (what we need to negotiate),
while I'm saying (what we need to negotiate).

1. Acknowledge agreement

We're both saying (what we agree upon) .

A New Way—Generating with Others

"A New Way" is a solution that goes beyond a combination of our initial positions. To generate "A New Way," we reason together. We align our brainpower to generate a new and better idea that we mutually agree upon.

Reasoning together is a process of mutual exploration, understanding, and action dedicated to generating "A New Way." Reasoning together includes *exploring* to determine mutually agreeable goals and working together to analyze the current situation. Reasoning involves *understanding* by expanding and narrowing together to develop new ideas. Reasoning culminates in *action* by planning, performing, and evaluating to test our new hypothesis. (These skills are more comprehensively presented later in this book in the chapter dedicated to reasoning skills.)

Merging with others to generate "A New Way" requires working through our reasoning processes together—mutual exploration, understanding, and action.

A New Way—Generating

> Reason together:
> - Mutual action
> - Mutual understanding
> - Mutual exploration

No Way—Fight, Flight, or Relate

"No Way" is neither "My Way," "Your Way," "Our Way," nor "A New Way." It is a breakdown in communications. It is an unwillingness to find common ground. It is the position of disconnected people. So what can we do when faced with this breakdown in communications? We will make some choices. We will choose from the basic responses of life: fight, flight, or relate.

When we choose to relate, we return to more attending, observing, listening, and responding. Somebody feels misunderstood. If we work at it enough, we will better understand their point of view. We may be able to communicate our understanding back to them so they feel understood. Then, they may be open to our initiatives and ideas. We may be able to return to merging our points of view—convincing, conceding, negotiating, or generating.

We may choose flight. Flight is a method of self-protection. If we assess that prolonged efforts to relate will not yield because of the other person's unwillingness or inability to relate, then we may decide to withdraw. We may decide that we do not want to lose "progress time." We are each free to decide, for ourselves, how we choose to invest our lives.

Lastly, we may choose to fight. We fight, only if we must, if we have no other possible course of action. Fighting is always a costly choice. In civilized cultures, we turn to the rule of law where we seek the judgment of arbiters, judges, or juries of our peers. In uncivilized situations, police must arrest those who choose physical fighting. In larger conflicts, the leaders of countries may determine that a military response is necessary. All fighting is terribly costly in resources and time, or even worse, as in times of war—in lives lost. Fighting is a last resort.

Experiencing someone else's "No Way" is not what anyone wants but it sometimes happens. When it does, we have choices: to relate and return to getting, giving, and merging; to flee or withdraw our presence; or to fight.

Summarizing Merging

The process of merging is a great opportunity for thinking with others. Merging, or "uniting to think together," results in one of the following: "My Way," "Your Way," "Our Way," or "A New Way." The processes of merging involve:

- **Convincing**—that "My Way" is the best way;

- **Conceding**—that "Your Way" is the best way;

- **Negotiating**—that "Our Way" is the preferred way; or

- **Generating**—that together we can create "A New Way" and it will be the best way.

The act of merging keeps us humble and makes us smart. We have so much to learn from each other. There is so much we can create together, but only if we are willing to merge or unite our brainpower.

A New Way—Generating

Reason together:
- Mutual action
- Mutual understanding
- Mutual exploration

Our Way—Negotiating

- Summarize negotiated agreement
- Negotiate differences
- Acknowledge agreement

My Way—Convincing

Improve my presentation.

Your Way—Conceding

Accept the other person's position.

The Benefits of Merging

How stringently we hold our position depends upon how important we think what we are showing and saying is for others. Authoritarian and totalitarian people expend their energies trying to control and direct everything, democratic people spend their energies trying to be inclusive of the ideas and information of others.

No one can control the thoughts of another person. What we can do is empower others with information that we believe is in their best interests, and they can do the same with us. There is much that we can learn from each other. We can stimulate and contribute to the development of new and better ideas! Everyone benefits from the skills of *The Inclusive Person.*

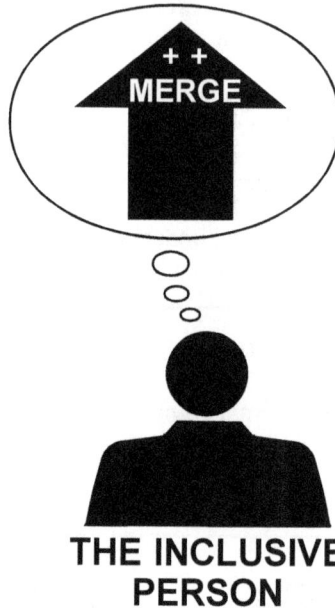

THE INCLUSIVE PERSON

Summarizing Relating

In summary, we relate by getting, giving, and merging our messages.

Getting begins by paying attention, observing, and listening to receive information, and culminates when we respond interchangeably to check the accuracy of what we think we saw and heard. These are the skills of *empathic relating*.

Giving means doing or physically modeling what we want to communicate, showing or visually presenting information, and telling or descriptively explaining our message in words. These are the skills we use to communicate new information to others. These are the skills of *additive relating*.

When **Merging**, we may convince others to accept "My Way" or concede to "Your Way" as best. We may acknowledge areas of agreement and negotiate our differences to develop "Our Way." We may align with others to mutually generate "A New Way." What is essential in our effort to merge with information and its authors is our willingness to embrace the inherent benefits of differing points of view. Differences are the source of our own new thinking! When we merge, we tolerate, include, and encourage ideas that are different from our own. These are the skills of *inclusive relating*.

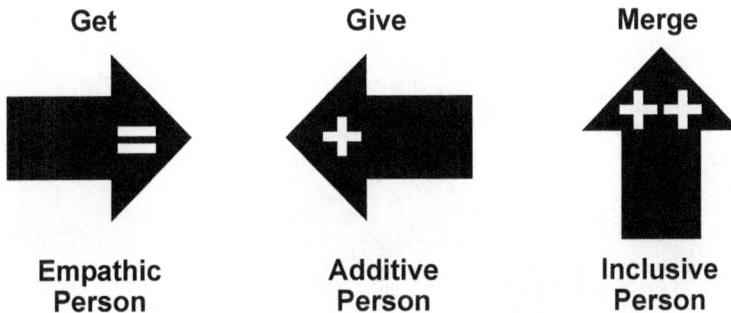

Get	Give	Merge
➡ =	⬅ +	⬆ ++
Empathic Person	**Additive Person**	**Inclusive Person**

The Benefits of Relating

Relating means getting, giving, and merging and results in empathic, additive, and inclusive relationships. Relating unlocks and discovers important information. Relating involves others with us as we go on to represent and reason to find currently available solutions to our problems and, better still, to create breakthrough ideas to benefit ourselves and others!

4

R²—Representing

Sentences, Systems, and Schematics

We learn or obtain information by relating or connecting with other people or other sources of information. The information we receive, however, may be incomplete or not organized in ways that are understandable or meaningful for us. The information that we communicate to others may sometimes have the same problems. When we are effective communicators, we organize and represent information to make it readily accessible and useful for ourselves and for others.

Information can be organized and represented in many different formats: cause-and-effect diagrams, entity diagrams with bubbles and arrows, flow charts, spider diagrams, and many more methods. We have concluded that there are three especially useful ways to organize and represent information. We have found outstanding benefits to generating new information when we use **sentences, systems,** and **schematics.**

(After reading this book, you may choose to analyze how these three methods for representing information can be used to help you understand the benefits and limitations of many other forms of information representation.)

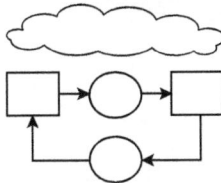

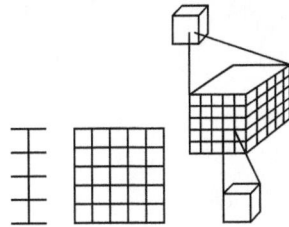

Sentences	Systems	Schematics
Articulate Reporter	Systems Scientist	Information Modeler

S¹ – Sentences

Sentences communicate information. Musicians represent their sentences with notes and musical notations. Mathematicians represent their sentences in equations. The most common sentences, however, are structured with words. Which words we choose and how we put them together tell a story.

The Language of Sentences

Since early childhood, we have been full of questions: What is that? Who is that? How does it work? Why is this being done? When and where does it take place? How well is it working? All our sentences ask or answer questions. A most useful method for organizing information is to ask and answer the **5W2H** interrogatives: *who, what, why, when, where, how,* and *how well.*

5W2H QUESTIONS

Who?
What?
Why?
When?
Where"
How?
How well?

Communicating with Sentences

To ask and answer questions, we use sentences. We use sentences to explain *facts*. We write or tell about *concepts* or how some facts relate to others. We can use sentences to explain *principles* or how and why things work. Our sentences tell about *applications* or when, where, and why these principles are put to use. We use sentences to communicate *objectives* or specific measures of performance. All our sentences are combinations of answers to the 5W2H interrogatives.

Here are some categories of information that we can communicate with sentences:

Objectives or **Measures of Performance**

Applications or **Uses**

Principles or **Processes**

Concepts or **Relationships**

Facts or **Labels**

Representing Facts. Facts are the labels or names we use to describe things. We use facts to answer all of the basic 5W2H questions:

- *Who* is involved?
- *What* are they doing?
- *Why* are they doing it?
- *When and where* is it being done?
- *How* are they doing it?
- *How well* are they doing it?

Whether at school or at home or at work, we often have problems to solve. When we remember to ask and answer all of the 5W2H questions we increase our chances for finding or creating a solution for our problem. When we forget to answer one of these 5W2H questions we may find that we have missed a fact that was essential for success. The 5W2H facts are building blocks for "Thinking with Sentences."

Here is a list of questions to help us remember how to be comprehensive in our communication of "facts:"

5W2H QUESTIONS

> **Who?**
>
> **What?**
>
> **Why?**
>
> **When?**
>
> **Where"**
>
> **How?**
>
> **How well?**

Representing Concepts. Concepts are relationships between facts. When we relate any two facts, we create a concept. For example, when we modify a noun with an adjective, we are creating a concept in the form of a phrase. When we join an adverb to an action word, we are building a concept, another phrase.

Concepts, or phrases, are partial sentences. Vivid phrases conjure vivid ideation. They engage us to imagine something. The more vivid the image that a phrase communicates, the more memorable it can be. If we cannot remember a concept or phrase we will not be able to build upon it for any practical purpose.

Effective communicators develop vivid, meaningful concepts with vivid, meaningful phrases. Yet, even an interesting mental image falls short of being comprehensive in its description. There is so much more we want to know that a good concept will not tell us. Concepts may provide more and better information than unrelated facts, but "principles" will tell us even more.

Here is a format for remembering "concepts:"

> When   who and what   ,
>
> then   what   .

Representing Principles. Principles are an explanation of processes or steps for how things work or how they relate. Principles can also include an explanation of why particular processes or steps work. We may need to use a series of sentences to explain a principle.

Finding out how things work and why they work is enlightening. Principles communicate important information for our consideration and stimulate our thinking. We can build additional information by asking and answering questions about applications or uses of information.

Here is a format to help us remember "principles:"

When	who and what	,
by	how and why	,
then	what	.

Representing Applications. Sentences can also tell about applications by explaining some specific uses of a principle or principles. Sentences about applications include specific information regarding when and where an activity has or will take place. Sentences about applications can also tell us why the activity is occurring. At the application level, sentences bring us information about utility or usefulness. We will usually need a series of sentences to explain specific applications.

Here is a format to help us remember "applications:"

When	who and what	,
by	how and why	,
then	what	,
so that	when, where, and why	.

Representing Objectives. Our growing assemblage of information can still be added to with more specificity—information about objectives or measures of performance. Objectives explain something that can be aimed towards or striven for. An objective explains how we can measure some factor(s) or feature(s) that we intend to accomplish. When we answer the question, "How well?" we describe what we are aiming towards or striving for. Writing or telling about objectives may also require a series of sentences.

Objectives provide information about measurements. When we measure things, we find out how much of an ingredient will make our facts, concepts, principles, and application information work. Asking and answering the "how well" measurement question may be the difference between knowing enough to make a difference or not—between outstanding success or utter failure.

This format can help us remember "objectives:"

When	who and what	,
by	how and why	,
then	what	,
so that	when, where, and why	,
as measured by	how well	.

Summarizing Sentences

Sentences are great communication tools. We use them to ask and answer questions. Sentences use words to create images for our imaginations. We then match these images with our life's experiences to construct ideas in our own minds. The construction of sentences is a work of creativity and, so too, is reading them or listening to them.

Historically, the role of journalists or reporters has been to go out and find the answers to all the questions they could think of. Then, their job was to be articulate, use "an economy of well-chosen words," and deliver the whole story. When we give information, this is our job too, to discover and communicate the whole truth, all of the 5W2H information. Are we comprehensive in our communication? Do we communicate answers to all of the 5W2H questions?

The test of our communication will be measured by the recipients of our message. Can others be interchangeable with us? Can they tell or show the 5W2H information we have said or written in sentences?

```
      5W2H
  ─────────────
  Who?    When?
  What?   Where?
  Why?    How?
     How well?
```

**THE ARTICULATE
REPORTER**

S² – Systems

Sentences are often not the most efficient way to communicate information. Sometimes other ways, like systems drawings, are more efficient and more useful. Systems drawings communicate information in a visual format that combines words with their relative positions within a drawing.

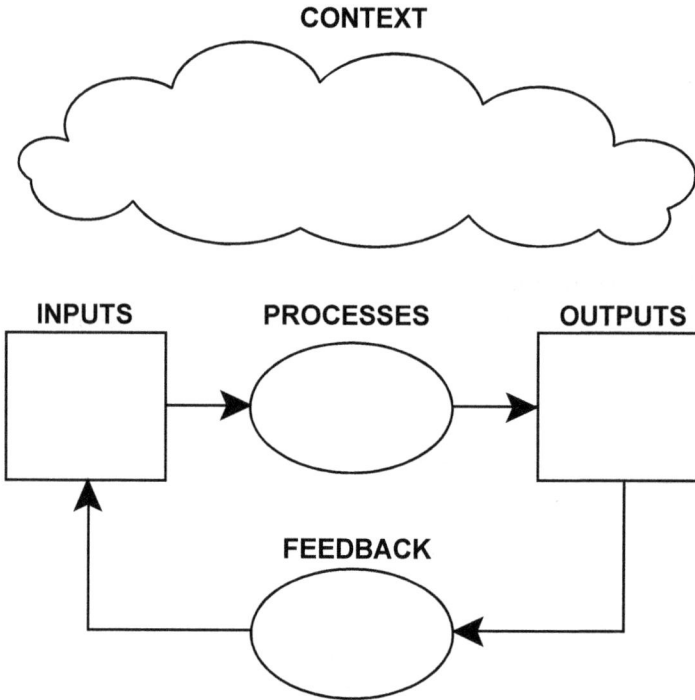

CONTEXT

INPUTS **PROCESSES** **OUTPUTS**

FEEDBACK

The Language of Systems

A systems drawing is a useful tool for representing complex information. A systems drawing can represent lots of information in a single drawing. A systems drawing shows five parts and how these parts relate to each other. The five parts of a systems drawing are outputs, inputs, processes, context, and feedback.

- **Results Outputs**
- **Resource Inputs**
- **Processes**
- **Conditions or Context**
- **Measures of Feedback or Metrics**

Communicating with Systems

We might know about systems. We might have studied the systems operating within our bodies: the respiratory, circulatory, skeletal, endocrine, nervous, and reproductive systems. Photosynthesis is a system. Some people have claimed to have a system for investing in the stock market or for predicting a winning horse at the racetrack. Some systems representations are more accurate than others.

When we represent systems we include information about the output or results we expect; the inputs or resources that are needed; the processes or activities that need to occur; the context or conditions within which the system operates; and the feedback information we measure that can be used to modify the system.

What is wonderful about a systems representation is that we get to see an overview explanation in a single picture. When we ask others to present their message in a systems drawing, we are asking them to "get specific." When others ask us to present our message in a systems drawing, they are asking us to "get specific" too. An avalanche of sentences may obfuscate or hide a message but there's no hiding with a systems drawing. With a systems drawing, we can see the parts and how they relate.

- **Results**
- **Resources**
- **Processes**
- **Conditions**
- **Feedback**

Representing Results Outputs. *Results outputs* tell **what** happens. They describe products that are produced or responses that are made. At work or in school, we might ask about outputs, "What do you expect to see when I've completed the task?" Teachers who are asking their learners to produce a particular result might model outputs by showing an exemplary product that is already completed; "Here is the kind of result I'd like you to produce." Outputs describe results. A useful first question for representing any system is "What is being produced here?"

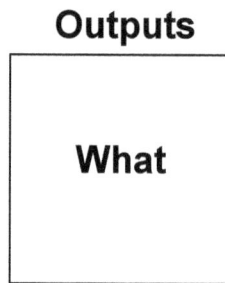

Outputs

```
┌─────────────┐
│             │
│   What      │
│             │
│             │
└─────────────┘
```

Representing Resource Inputs. *Resource inputs* tell **who** and **what** is required to get **what** results. Resource inputs are needed to get results outputs. At work, we might ask resource questions like "Who will be working on this and what other resources will be available for this project?" For a school project we might ask similar resource questions of our teacher and of ourselves: "Who and what will I need to help me complete this assignment?"

If we listed the results outputs we are looking for and the resource inputs we think we will need, we have the start of a systems diagram and a useful way to communicate information.

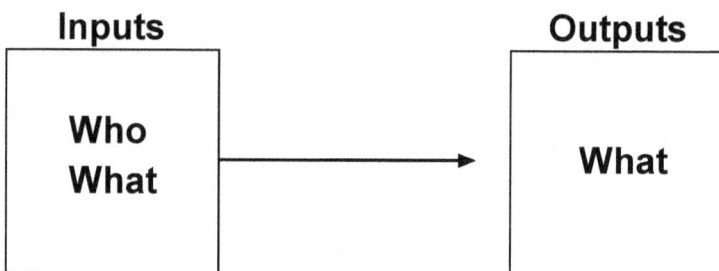

Inputs   **Outputs**

```
┌─────────────┐                    ┌─────────────┐
│             │                    │             │
│   Who       │──────────────────▶ │   What      │
│   What      │                    │             │
│             │                    │             │
└─────────────┘                    └─────────────┘
```

Representing Processes. *Processes* are the events that take resources and transform them into results. Processes are the actions or activities of change. Processes tell **how** and **why** things change. Processes are a series of step-by-step behaviors, and may also ask and answer **why** these specific processes are effective.

By charting inputs, processes, and outputs (I, P, O) we are building an overview graphic of our system. Already we can show this information to others and get their feedback and their ideas to help us improve our system.

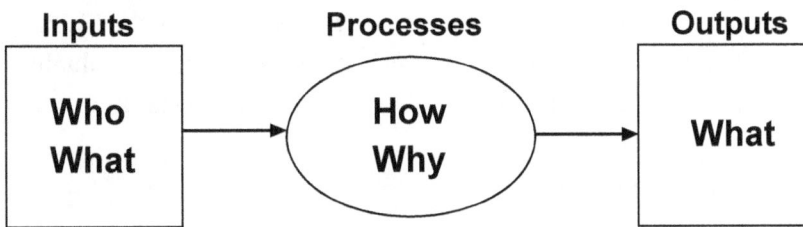

Inputs	Processes	Outputs
Who **What**	**How** **Why**	**What**

Representing *Contexts* or *Conditions*. The *conditions* or *contexts* of a system tell **when** and **where** the inputs will be transformed into outputs. In other words, contextual information tells us **when** and **where** the system is, or will be, applied or used. Information about place (where) and time (when) helps us visualize the system in actual operation.

Contextual information, most importantly, tells us *why* this system exists. Why do we want this system? What benefits will be accrued from accomplishing the outputs? Contextual information provides a perspective. It tells us that our system is in service of a bigger condition or context, a more important purpose.

The listing of contextual information, place, time, and purpose of the system, presents important information for further discussion and thinking.

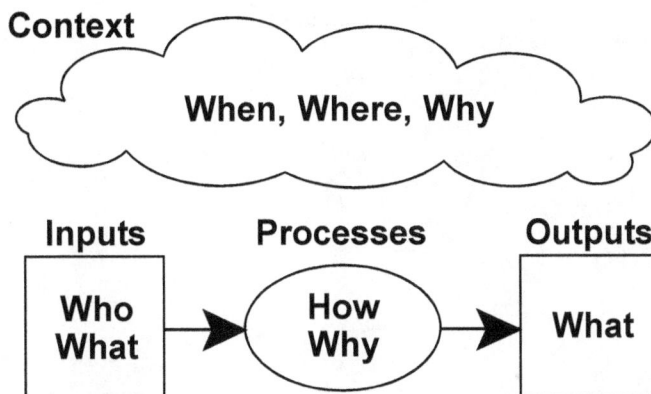

Context

When, Where, Why

Inputs	Processes	Outputs
Who **What**	**How** **Why**	**What**

Representing Metrics or Measured Feedback. *Feedback* answers **how well.** We answer the how well question by first selecting what we want to measure. Although we may ask the how well question about the *processes* or the *resource inputs,* the most common use of feedback is to represent how we measure our *results outputs.*

To answer the *how well* question, we must select or devise quantitative and qualitative metrics (measures) of whatever part of the system for which we are seeking feedback information. Feedback is about evaluating the quality and quantity of the parts of our system.

Now we have a complete systems design. Once we answer the 5W2H questions and place our answers within a systems diagram, we have a valuable representation of current information to stimulate new and still better information.

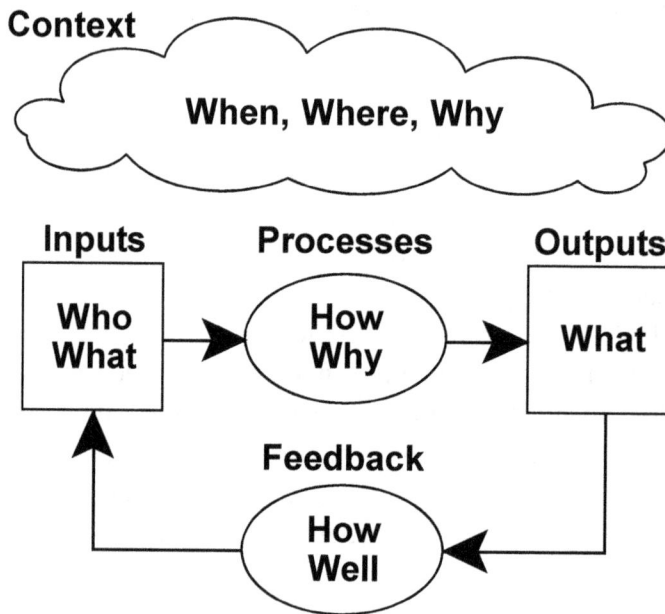

Context

When, Where, Why

Inputs	Processes	Outputs
Who What	**How Why**	**What**

Feedback

How Well

Summarizing Systems

Systems diagrams help us clarify our thinking. When we ask ourselves to present our ideas as a system, we ask ourselves to explain our view as simply and as powerfully as we can. With a systems drawing, others can also show us their understanding of the parts of an idea and how the parts relate. Systems diagrams help us see the system as a whole and stimulate us to think about individual parts of the system. Systems diagrams are outputs of, and inputs to, thinking!

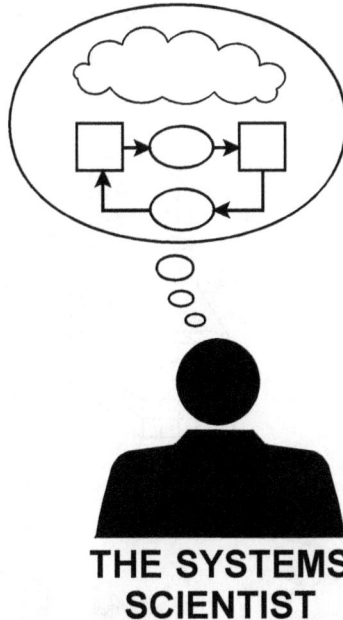

THE SYSTEMS SCIENTIST

S³ – Schematics

Words are the basic units of sentences. Words positioned within a systems diagram are the basic units of systems. Words and how they are positioned along axes or dimensions are the building blocks of what we call "schematics." Schematics present information along "x," "y," "z" or "nested" axes. By doing this, we can look at how the information on one axis interacts with the information on another axis or dimension.

Schematics help us to define our ideas and represent them in a way that we can see them and think about them. We will see that there is valuable information that would escape our attention if we did not represent it schematically or dimensionally (along axes).

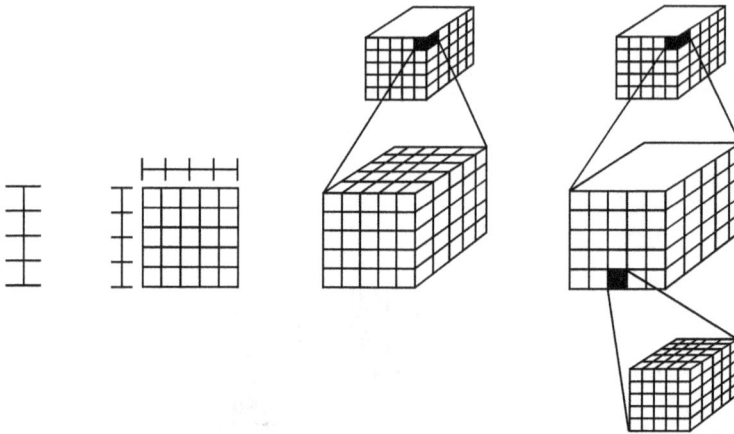

The Language of Schematics

We are "information modelers." We write sentences, make systems drawings, or use other methods to store and sort information. One such useful method is schematic or dimensional modeling. To help us sort and represent the dimensions of our schematic drawings, five terms are useful: functions, components, processes, conditions, and standards. We introduce these terms because they are commonly used in both science and business. These terms have a similar meaning as the five systems diagram terms: outputs, inputs, processes, contexts and feedback measures.

- **Functions** are words we use to describe what we want to result from some activity. (Outputs)

- **Components** are the parts, participants, or ingredients that will be needed to accomplish our desired functions or results. (Inputs)

- **Processes** are procedures or a series of steps that interact with components to accomplish functions. (Processes)

- **Conditions** are contexts that enable or restrict the interaction of components, functions, and processes. (Contexts)

- **Standards** are measures that we can use to compare actual performance with intended performance. (Feedback measures)

On the pages that follow, we will use these five terms as we organize, represent, and learn from schematic or dimensional information. (If you prefer, you can use the terms outputs, inputs, processes, contexts, and feedback measures.)

Communicating with Schematics

When we model information schematically, we use any of five methods for representing information by its dimensions (D): 1D scales, 2D matrices, 3D models, nested 3D models, and multi-nested 3D models. A **scale** is a series of words or phrases that share a common attribute and are organized in a line from low to high (ranking scale) or from first to last (sequenced scale). **Matrices** interact the words we place along two lines. Matrices show the interaction of two scales. A **3D model** is the interaction of three axes or scales. A **nested 3D model** shows how one 3D model can "nest" or reside inside another 3D model. A **multi-nested model** presents the additional nesting of 3D models. We will see that all of these methods of schematic modeling are useful tools for us.

- Multi-Nested 3D Model
- Nested 3D Model
- 3D Model
- 2D Matrix
- 1D Scale

Representing with Scales
(Ranking Scales or Sequence Scales)

A scale is "a series of marks along a line used to measure something" (*Webster's Dictionary*). To make a scale, we need to do two things. First, we have to decide *what* we want to measure. Second, we need to decide on *how* we can best measure it.

Here are two basic kinds of scales. One is a scale that displays a **ranking** of items (low to high) and the other displays a **sequence** of items (first to last). A thermometer is a good example of a scale that shows ranking. It measures temperature along a range from a low number to a high one. The ABC steps for CPR (cardio-pulmonary resuscitation), as recommended in 2008 by the Mayo Clinic (see scale below), is a good example of a scale that shows a sequence from first to last. A sequence scale is an ordering of steps to accomplish a task or a goal.

Scales are useful tools for presenting information. Ranking scales, for example, are an important tool for measuring functions or outputs. Ranking scales are also useful for measuring component inputs and system conditions. Sequence scales are useful for representing processes. We can use scaling to help us to discover and even create new information.

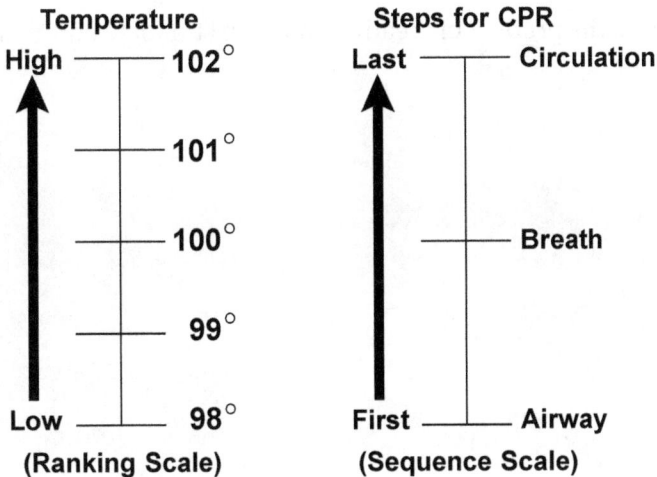

Temperature
High ——— 102°
——— 101°
——— 100°
——— 99°
Low ——— 98°
(Ranking Scale)

Steps for CPR
Last ——— Circulation
——— Breath
First ——— Airway
(Sequence Scale)

Representing with a Ranking Scale

We can measure anything. If it is important to us, we will devise a way to measure it. We will figure out a way to "count" whether it is "fully present" or "absent" at the extreme ends of our scale. We will find a way to count "how much" of it is found between these extremes.

To make a scale, we begin by deciding what we want to think about. We do this by asking questions of ourselves or others. As we think about what is important to us—what might make a difference or what might be effective—our questions and answers need to become more specific. We need to decide on an ingredient, an attribute, a construct, a feature, something that, if we have more of it, it will help solve our problem or, alternatively, if we have less of it our problem will worsen. Choosing which ingredient, attribute, construct, or feature we want is the basis for solving problems and creating opportunities. When we select some ingredient that we have never before considered for this purpose, we will find ourselves involved in the creative process.

Next, we will need to decide how we can measure it. Measurements are made through our senses and are sometimes extended and enhanced by the use of specialized tools like the microscope, electronic sensors, chemical dyes, or many other tools.

A new scale is the product of creativity and can stimulate additional creativity.

Representing with a Ranking Scale
(Rating with Tools)

To make a ranking scale, we begin by following the simple two steps of scaling. Choose **what** to measure and **how** we want to measure it.

People in the field of health, for example, measure things like the percentage of saturated fat in foods, weight in pounds or kilograms, and blood pressure measured in number of heartbeats per minute. Although we may collect data about the percentage of fat in a particular food, a weight measurement or a blood pressure reading, what gives meaning to each of these facts is their relative position along a scale. We need to see our information along a continuum or scale to begin to understand its meaning for us.

Scaling information along a continuum gets us thinking about what we are measuring. Scaling makes us ask questions about what constitutes higher performance and lower performance. Scaling delivers "perspective" so we can aim higher and perform better.

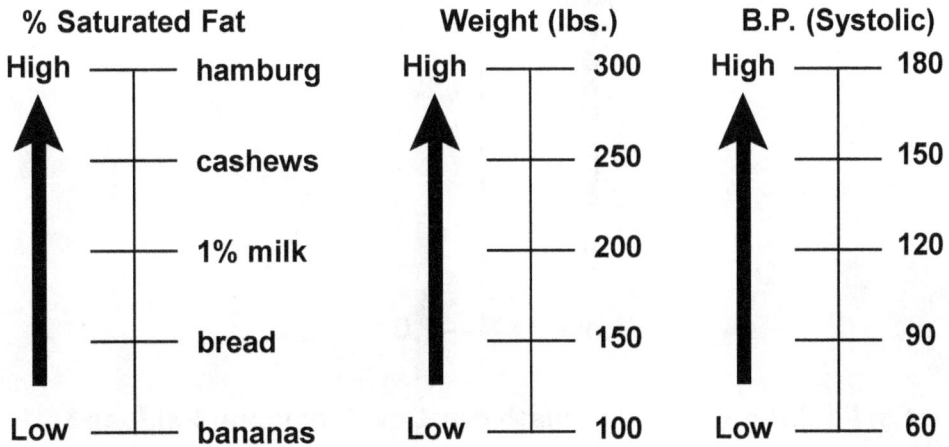

% Saturated Fat	Weight (lbs.)	B.P. (Systolic)
High — hamburg	High — 300	High — 180
cashews	250	150
1% milk	200	120
bread	150	90
Low — bananas	Low — 100	Low — 60

Representing with a Ranking Scale
(Rating a Behavior)

Here is an example of a ranking scale being built. We are having an interpersonal communications problem. We do some research and find out that if more "empathy" is expressed between the parties, then communications will improve. "Empathy" is the ingredient that we want to scale. Now, we get specific about how we know when we have lots of empathy present or not. We will make "frequency counts"—the more often we hear an empathic "interchangeable response," the more empathy is present.

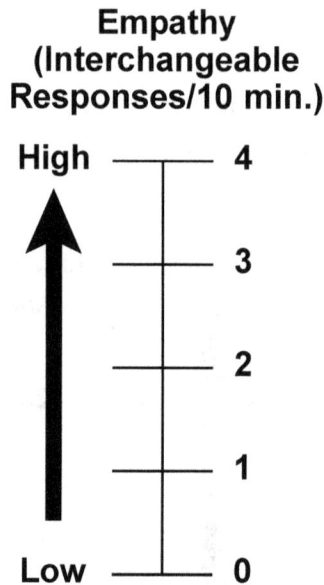

**Empathy
(Interchangeable
Responses/10 min.)**

High ——— **4**

——— **3**

——— **2**

——— **1**

Low ——— **0**

Special Ranking Scale: "Cumulative or Developmental Ranking Scale".
One special kind of ranking scale is called a "cumulative ranking scale" or "developmental ranking scale."

A "cumulative ranking scale" or "developmental ranking scale" simply means that the higher levels of the scale include the lower levels. With a cumulative ranking scale, a measurement of performance at the highest level of a scale means that all the levels below it were also accomplished—they "accumulate" or are "cumulative." A development ranking scale simply means that in order to reach a higher level, we pass through the lower levels.

Here is an example of a cumulative or developmental scale for "Interdependent Relating."

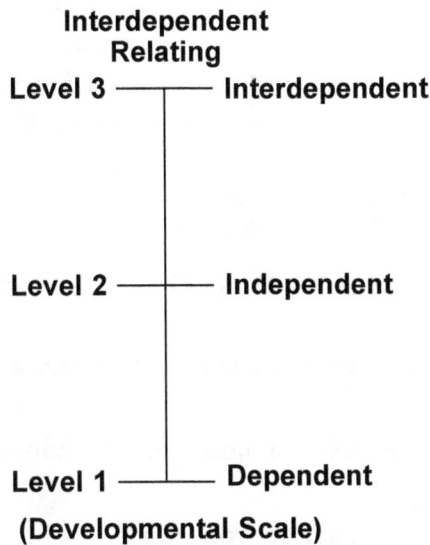

Interdependent Relating

Level 3 ———— Interdependent

Level 2 ———— Independent

Level 1 ———— Dependent

(Developmental Scale)

Special Ranking Scale: "Threshold Ranking Scale". Another special ranking scale is a "threshold ranking scale." To create a threshold ranking scale, we begin by identifying the middle rating, a rating of acceptable performance—the performance threshold. Below this measurement is "not acceptable." Above the threshold measurement is superior performance (> threshold).

An example of a threshold ranking scale is a scale about how much we are saving each year for our children's college tuition or for retirement.

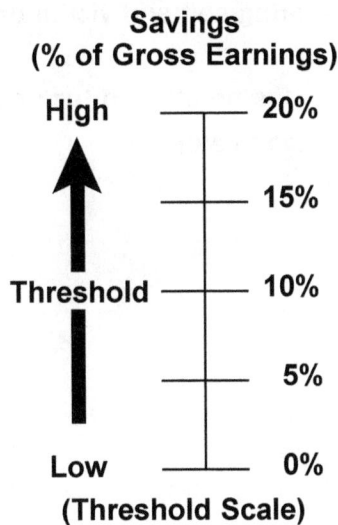

**Savings
(% of Gross Earnings)**

High ———— 20%

———— 15%

Threshold ———— 10%

———— 5%

Low ———— 0%

(Threshold Scale)

Representing with a Sequence Scale

Here are two examples of sequence scales or first-to-last scales. This kind of scale is a way to describe a series of steps to a goal. A sequence scale is a chronological plan of action. To make a scale to overview a process, we list and measure the main action steps. If we want to communicate more detailed information, we may decide to make an additional, more detailed sub-scale.

**Steps for Escape
and Swimming Rescue**

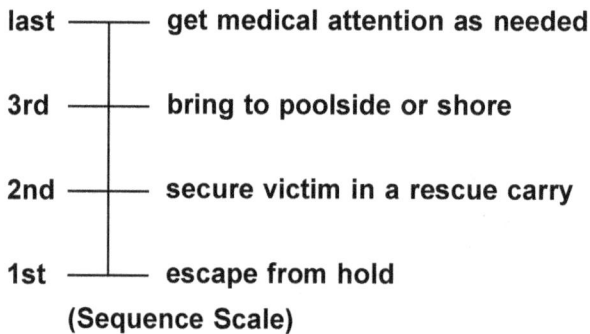

last ——— get medical attention as needed

3rd ——— bring to poolside or shore

2nd ——— secure victim in a rescue carry

1st ——— escape from hold
(Sequence Scale)

Escape from Hold

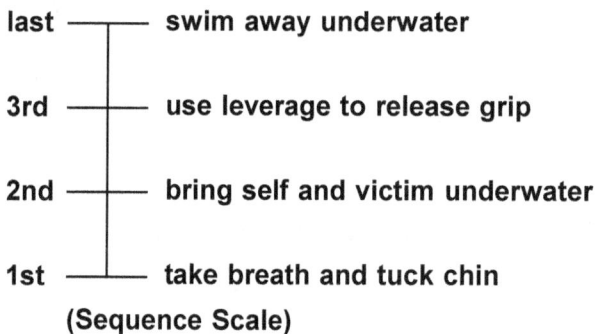

last ——— swim away underwater

3rd ——— use leverage to release grip

2nd ——— bring self and victim underwater

1st ——— take breath and tuck chin
(Sequence Scale)

The Benefits of Scales

What Scales Can Do for Us. Scales are a product of thinking. Instead of simply "doing what we've always done in the past," we ask ourselves to think about what we "want to do" and "what we think will work." We are thinking when we hypothesize what performance will make a difference. We are thinking when we create a rating scale (low to high) to measure performance. We are thinking when we generate a sequence scale (first to last).

Scales measure performance. With a ranking scale, we can measure how well we are performing. With a sequencing scale, we can outline our action plan, see what we have accomplished, and what else needs to be done.

Are our scales useful? Are they valid? Are they reliable? Are we measuring what will work or are we fooling ourselves? Are we working on an effective plan or are we shoveling sand into the ocean? Without a scale, or some other means of communicating our performance and our processes, we will never know.

The scales we generate are our hypotheses about life. With each scale we take a stand, ever willing to change them based on the feedback of experience. When we find our scales to be inaccurate we will abandon them, modify them, or generate new ones. Our scales represent our hypotheses. We must make them before we can test them. We will use scales to define our goals and measure our successes. Remember the truism, "You get what you measure." Scales are tools for measurement.

Representing with a Matrix

A matrix is a set of numbers or words that are arranged in rows and columns. Tables are another word we use to describe matrices. Many math and science problems require us to build matrices or tables. Tables and matrices are commonly found in textbooks, magazines, and newspapers. "Spreadsheet" software programs allow users to build information into a two-dimensional (2D) format of columns and rows (tables or matrices). Being able to read and build spreadsheets, tables, and matrices are standard skills for learning and working in today's world.

The most common 2D matrix we can build interacts two lists. If the items in each list are randomly ordered, when we present the interaction of the two lists we may not be especially enlightened by what we see. When we interact two scales, however, we begin to see patterns that can be informative and useful for us and for others. Matrices are valuable tools for learning, thinking, and creating. Matrices can interact any dimension of information with any other dimension of information: functions, components, processes, conditions, or standards.

NOTE: These next few pages introduce the reader to 3D information models, nested-3D information models, and multi-nested 3D information models. They are worthy of a book themselves, with lots of examples. You may decide to read about them here, or not. We just wanted you to know of their existence and, perhaps, in the future you may be interested in learning how to represent information with these modeling methods. You may decide to skip these few pages if you prefer, go on to the summary about Schematics, and then continue with the next chapter on Reasoning.

Representing with a 3D Model

We can begin thinking about a 3D model as simply adding one more dimension to a 2D matrix. When three dimensions of information are represented together, we see a cube or block of information. A 3D model can interact any dimension of information with any other dimension of information: functions, components, processes, conditions, or standards.

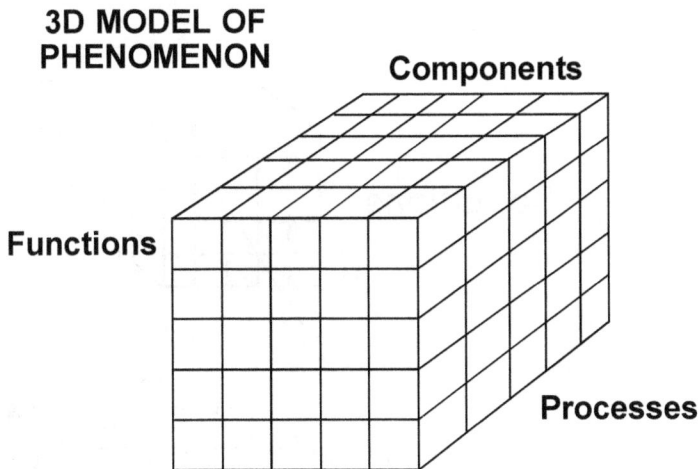

3D MODEL OF PHENOMENON

Components

Functions

Processes

The interaction of scales has much more potential meaning for us than the interaction of lists. In our experience, we have found that 3D models are especially meaningful when we interact functions or results we want, with components or parts or participants, with processes or steps for change. We call this kind of 3D model of information a "model of phenomenon," because this interaction of information is "life-like" in that we have represented its parts, its intentions, and its processes. This 3D information model will help us to learn, think, and create in relation to it.

Representing with Nested-3D Model

A nest is "a cozy or snug place in which to live or rest" (*Webster's Dictionary*). We build nested models as representations of places where one model lives or rests or resides within another. It is obvious to all of us that some phenomena can be thought of as nested inside other phenomena. Our brains are nested in our bodies. Our classrooms are nested in our schools. Our schools are nested within our communities and on and on.

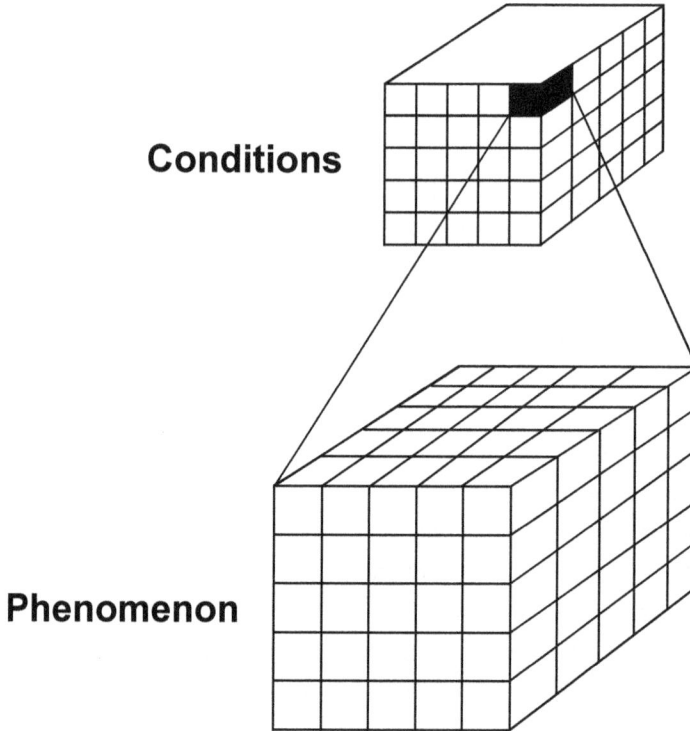

Conditions

Phenomenon

When we think of a nest within which a phenomenon lives, we can think of it as the context or conditions within which the phenomenon operates. We can model these relationships. We represent a nested model by showing how one phenomenon provides the context or conditions for another phenomenon. In our experience, we use the term *conditions* to define the larger 3D model within which the smaller model, the 3D phenomenal model, operates. As we use our brainpower to define and build a bigger contextual model, we will begin to see how it impacts upon a smaller, nested one. By building contextual models to nest smaller ones we begin to see information with a perspective we previously were not privileged to see.

Representing with Multi-Nested 3D Models

Take nesting one step further. Think about smaller models that can help us to explain what is going on in bigger ones. This time we are looking inside our phenomenal model to determine what's going on. We can build another model within any intersection of information in the original phenomenal model if it is something we want to think about. In our experience, we use the term *standards* to define the smaller 3D model that is nested within the 3D phenomenal model. When we build this nested model we can begin to see how the little model can be used to help us measure performance in the bigger model. Once again, we may gain a perspective that was previously unavailable to us and our thinking.

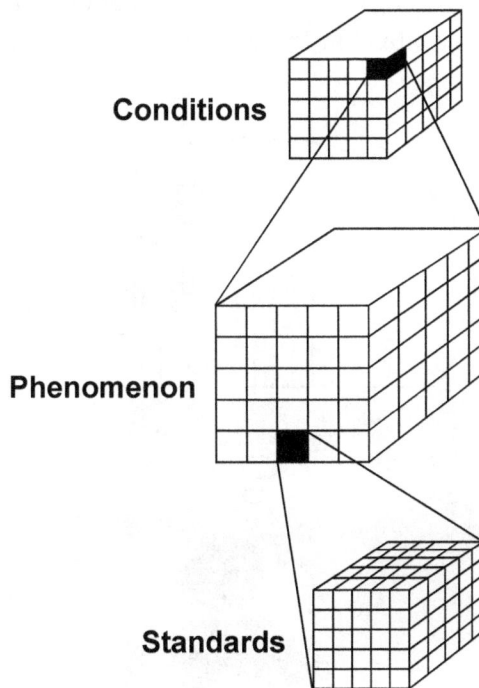

Conditions

Phenomenon

Standards

Summarizing Schematics

We use the term *schematics* to mean how we represent and relate the dimensions of information. Our schematic diagrams include 1D scales, 2D matrices, 3D models, nested 3D models, and multi-nested 3D models.

Schematic representations are tools for learning, thinking, and creating. The more we use schematics to model information, the more we will come to understand and appreciate its usefulness. By asking ourselves to use schematics to model information, we are asking ourselves to clarify our ideas.

We need not do all our thinking on our own. We can get others to work with us. But first, we might need to teach them how to build scales and matrices, and maybe even models. By asking others to use schematics to model information we will be asking them to elevate their thinking to levels that they have never before been empowered to achieve.

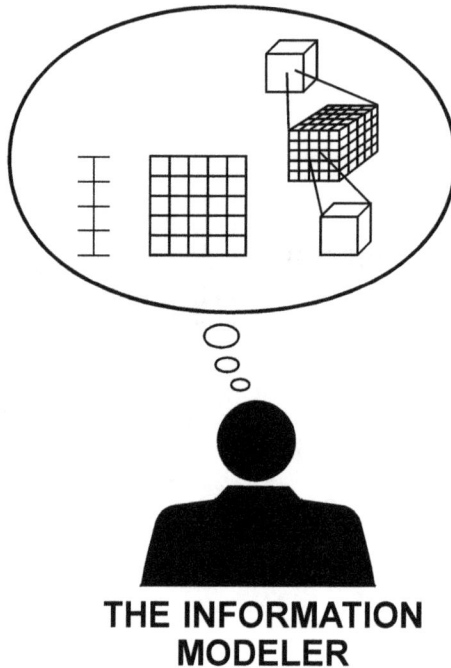

THE INFORMATION MODELER

Summarizing Representing

In summary, we represent information with sentences, systems, and schematics.

We may choose to use **sentences** to tell our stories. All of our sentences explain answers to the basic interrogatives, the 5W2H questions. Our sentences explain facts, concepts, and principles. They describe applications and define objectives. We can all be *articulate reporters* of information.

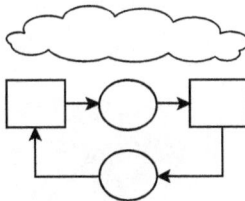

Sometimes we choose to represent information by using a **systems** drawing. Here we combine words with their relative positions within a diagram of a system. Our system diagrams show us resources and results and the processes that transform them. They show us measures of feedback and the conditions or context of the system. We can all be *systems scientists.*

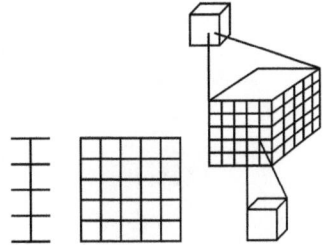

Schematics present information along axes and then show the interactions of this information. Schematics present information as 1D scales, 2D matrices, 3D models, nested 3D models, and multi-nested 3D models. We can all become *information modelers.*

Representing with sentences, systems, and schematics results in articulate reporting, systems perspectives, and information models.

Sentences	Systems	Schematics
Articulate Reporter	**Systems Scientist**	**Information Modeler**

5
R³—Reasoning

Ready for Reasoning

We have learned about **relating** with information and people who produce it. We know when we are following systematic relating methods and when we are not. Now we can challenge ourselves to skillfully **get, give,** and **merge**.

We learned about **representing** information with **sentences, systems,** and **schematics**. We understand that the power of ideas is significantly impacted by the methods we use for representing them. We have learned useful methods for representing ideas, and now we can internalize these methods as new standards for what we will require of our own representations and communications of information. We can now also elevate our standards for assessing the representations of ideas that we will read about and hear about from others. We will notice what information is there and what is missing.

Our skills for **relating** and **representing** will serve us well as we apply our brainpower to **reasoning**.

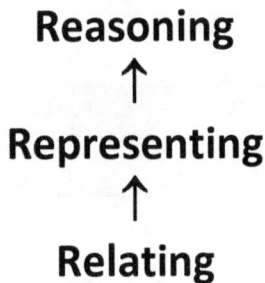

Reasoning
↑
Representing
↑
Relating

List of My Reasoning Skill Steps

We already know something about reasoning. It's a term we have often heard: "Let's be reasonable," "We'll reason this out," "Let me tell you my reasons for this decision." Yet, what do we mean by the term *reasoning?* If we asked ourselves to show and tell the methodologies or steps we use when we reason, what would they be? In other words, how do we represent the skills of reasoning?   Here is some extra help in defining the skills of reasoning. *Webster's Dictionary* defines reasoning with the phrases "a process for explaining or justifying a cause or motive," "the ability to systematically think," "analyze information," "draw conclusions," and "form judgments." These phrases may help you to expand your own descriptions of the skills you use when you reason.

Take some time and analyze your own vision of reasoning. Write down the steps you take when you reason. Make this self-analysis before you go ahead and see how the skills in this chapter can help you succeed in becoming a more creative and free person.

Go ahead, think about how you reason and write out the steps you take when working to solve a problem or create an opportunity.

_____

_____

_____

_____

_____

_____

_____

_____

Skills for Reasoning

Here are five sets of skills that we have found to be essential to reasoning: **goal-setting, analyzing, expanding, narrowing,** and **performing.** Did your list of reasoning skills include these steps?

We all know something about each of these sets of skills, yet how we define each of these skill sets, and how well we accomplish each one, will determine how well we reason.

- **Goal-Setting**

- **Analyzing**

- **Expanding**

- **Narrowing**

- **Performing**

EUA—Exploring, Understanding, and Acting

Overview of Reasoning Skills

To help us learn about and use these skill-sets for reasoning, we will start by organizing them so they become easier to remember. One way of describing the skills of reasoning is by using the acronym **EUA** and the terms **Exploring, Understanding,** and **Acting**.

By **exploring**, we explore information to see it for what it currently is (analysis), explore our own intentions in relation to information (set goals), and we expand to generate new visions of what might be possible.

By **understanding**, we innovate or generate a vision we can apply. We show our understanding by narrowing possibilities and potential into testable hypotheses.

Finally, by **acting** we transform potential into reality (plan, perform, and evaluate). In other words, we "bridge the gap" between a new "ideal or proposed possible" and a new "actual."

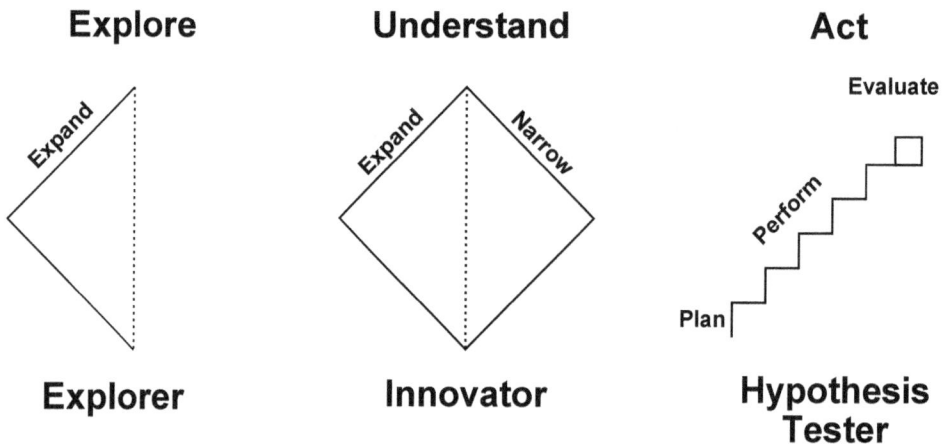

Explore	**Understand**	**Act**

Expand

Expand   Narrow

Evaluate

Perform

Plan

Explorer	**Innovator**	**Hypothesis Tester**

Exploring—Goal-Setting, Analyzing, and Expanding

We can think of ourselves as explorers. The idea of living life as an explorer is an exciting vision. It conjures thoughts of travel to places we have never before visited. As an explorer, we may travel to remote places where few have ever dared go to before. We may even find that our exploration leads to new discoveries. When we initiate reasoning by exploring information, we will prepare ourselves by examining the information carefully. Emotionally and intellectually, we enter or climb inside the information, so to speak. We become its traveling companion.

The skills of exploration include goal-setting, analysis, and expanding. Our goal is our reason for exploring. Analysis is our process for directing and recording our exploration of how things currently work. Expanding is our process for generating new visions of what may be possible.

When we explore, we will expand our goals or intentions, our analyses of current operations, and new options or possibilities. Exploring can be summarized as expanding to generate new possibilities.

**Set Goal, Analyze,
and Expand**

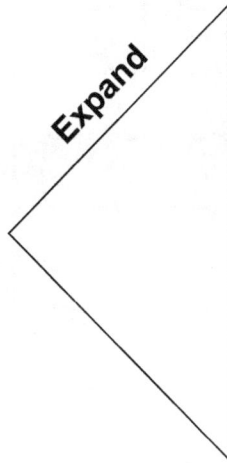

Goal-Setting—Problems and Opportunities

Goal setting begins with orienting or aiming ourselves towards whatever is important to us. What do we need to think about? What do we want to think about? What do we *want and need to think about?*

When we choose to be observers of life, we sit back and watch. We are members of the "audience." We may be taking in the experiences of others but we have nearly no impact upon what is happening.

When we choose to actively engage ourselves with the world around us, however, we experience what is happening as **problems** to be solved and/or **opportunities** to become involved with.

Our goals are defined by how we see ourselves in relation to problems and opportunities. We can begin to define our goals by listing problems or opportunities we want and need to think about. When we prioritize our lists, some items will rise to the top of our attention and our intentions. This item will head our "to do" list for thinking.

List of Goals
(Problems and/or Opportunities)

1.
2.
3.
4.
5.

Goal-Setting—Requirements and Values

Now that a specific problem or opportunity has our attention, we begin to take a closer look at it. We will find two sources of information about it—**internal values** and **external requirements**.

Our **values** are what we deem important to us. Our values are based upon the assumptions or hypotheses we have about how the world works and how we believe it could work better.

Requirements come from others and from the world around us.

Reasoning involves information from both our internal values and external requirements upon us. Ultimately, when we reason we take both of these sources of information into consideration before generating hypotheses and testing them for their validity and utility.

Goal-Setting

Problem or Opportunity _____
_____

Values	Requirements

Goal-Setting—Requirements x Values

Sometimes our goals seem simple. We quickly know what we want to accomplish (values) and what needs to be done (requirements). In an instant we may choose our intention and direction and act upon them immediately. We apply this abbreviated and efficient approach to reasoning when we drive a car and for many other tasks that require an immediate response. Hopefully, we have reasoned through these choice points in greater depth at some earlier time so we are prepared to make quick, yet reasoned, decisions.

All reasoning, however abbreviated, involves considering both internal values and external requirements.

VALUES

	Low	Moderate	High
High			✓
Moderate			
Low			

REQUIREMENTS

Exploring by Analyzing Sentences, Systems, and Schematics

Sometimes our goals are not so simple. We realize that the problem or opportunity we are faced with seems complex and not so well understood. We may have a general idea about what we want and need to do, but we want to think about it some more before deciding what action to take.

In the face of seeming complexity, we need to explore our goals and analyze situations in more depth. We begin our analysis by representing information in **sentences**, with **systems** diagrams, or with **schematics**. These methods for representing information will help us define what we know and what we don't yet know but will need to learn or generate.

Goal Setting and Analyzing with Schematics

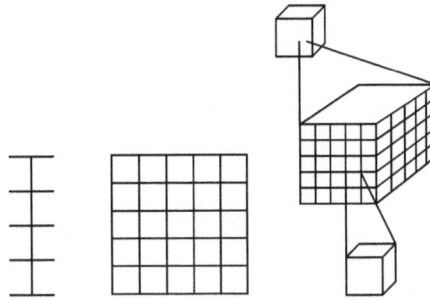

Goal Setting and Analyzing with Systems

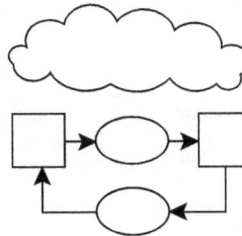

Goal Setting and Analyzing with Sentences

Analyzing with Sentences

We may comprehensively analyze our goals and our situation using words in sentences. A comprehensive analysis with sentences will answer all of the 5W2H interrogatives: who, what, when, where, why, how, and how well. The answers to these questions result in a comprehensive description of our current goal and the current situation (problems and opportunities).

If we cannot answer some of these questions, then we will have to do research to find answers. Sometimes there are no adequate answers to be found. Discovering missing or inadequate information shows us areas where we may want to focus our creative/generative energies.

When... _____(Who and What)_____

by..._____(How and Why)_____

then... _____(What)_____

so that... _____(When, Where and Why)_____

as measured by... _____(How Well)_____

Analyzing with Systems

When we complete an analysis by using a systems diagram, we will be able to see how resources are transformed into results. We will also see the conditions or context which impact the system. Additionally, we will show how the system parts are measured.

Any systems information that we cannot find, or we find inadequate, is an opportunity for further analysis and for our own creativity and generativity.

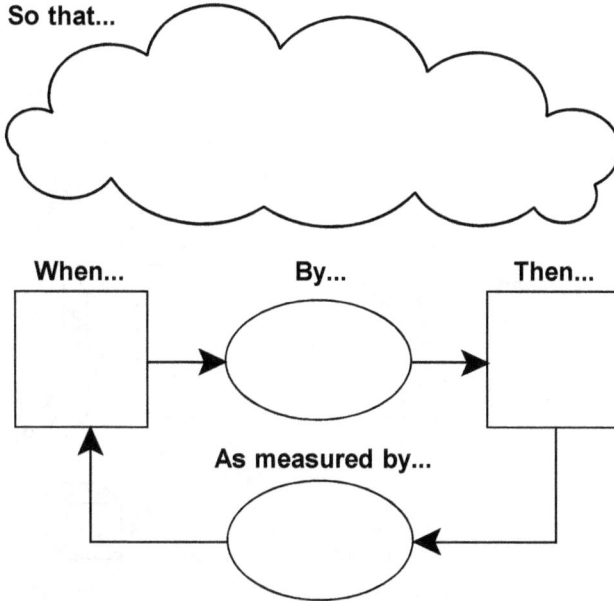

So that...

When...   **By...**   **Then...**

As measured by...

Analyzing with Schematics

A schematic analysis can result in still better information and most of all provides new perspectives. Each time we analyze information and put it in a scale, we are either ranking information (low to high) or sequencing information (first to last). A matrix interacts two scales. Models and nested models show the interaction of multiple scales and so offer additional information perspectives.

The use of scales, matrices, and models will reveal opportunities for further analysis and generative thinking.

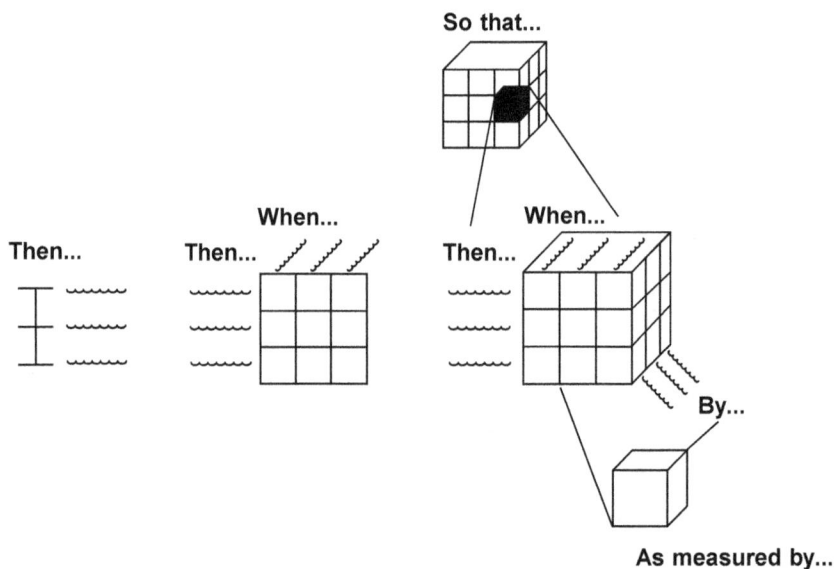

Analyzing the Current and Building the Possible

When we are disciplined in using sentences, systems, or schematics to explore our goals and analyze information, we will find that two different representations begin to emerge.

The first representation of information shows how things are right now. It is our "current view."

The next representation goes beyond the first in that it includes information that is not part of the current view. It includes new information and orients us to new areas of interest, study, and creativity. This is the start of our "possibilities view."

Often, we will find that parts of the current view are accurate and useful, and that they are a sub-set of the "possibilities view" we are building. Already, we are beginning to discover and create a new vision of the possible!

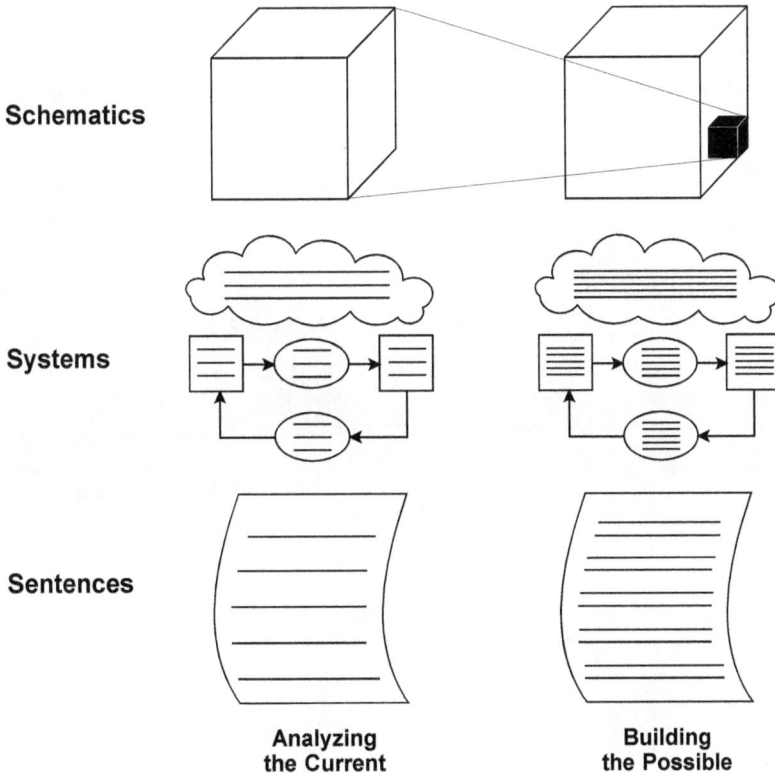

Schematics

Systems

Sentences

Analyzing the Current   **Building the Possible**

Exploring by Expanding

When we analyze information, we see it for what it currently is. When we apply the skills of **expanding** information, we will also see this same information for what it can become. If we want to use our abilities to reason beyond what is currently known, however, we must be willing to think beyond what is presented to us. Exploring means envisioning the possible by **expanding** to generate new possible options and alternatives.

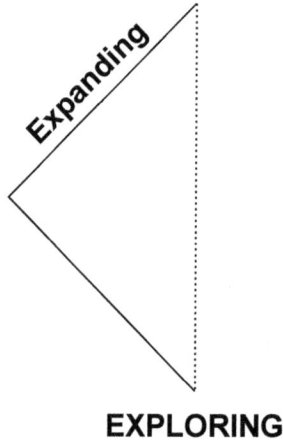

EXPLORING

Expanding with Sentences, Systems, and Schematics

Expanding is not a random process. We bring an organization to our process for expanding by using what we know about sentences, systems and schematics.

- When we expand by **using sentences,** we generate alternative answers to the 5W2H questions.

- When we expand our **systems drawing,** we look at our systems and consider alternatives that expand or replace the ingredients or relationships in our system.

- When we expand our **schematic representations,** we develop alternatives to the ingredients or dimensions of our schemas.

When we expand, we generate alternatives that will modify our sentences, systems, or schematics.

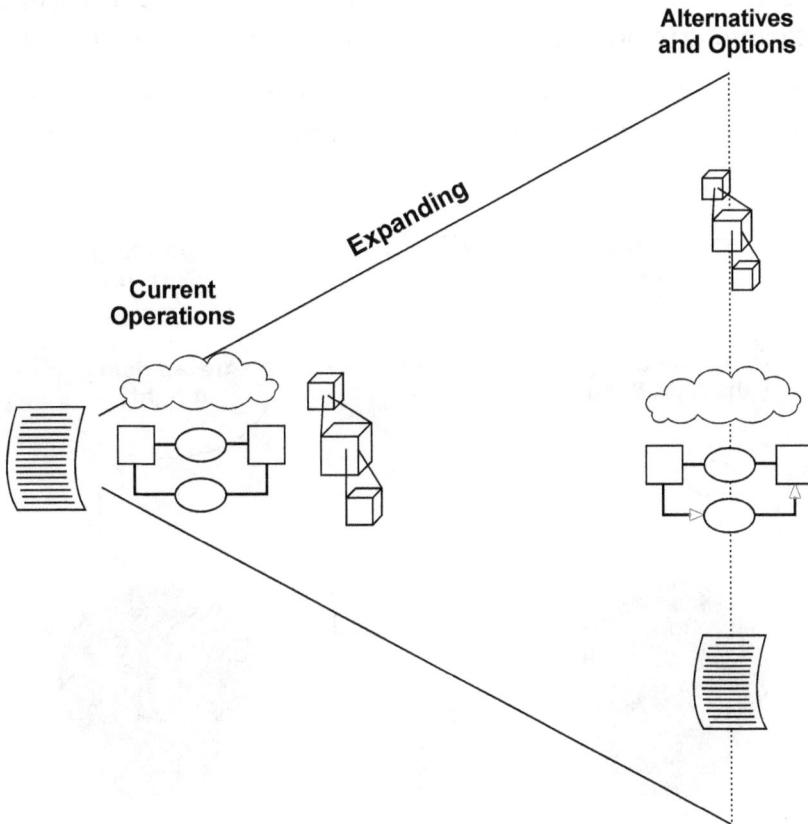

Expanding Beyond and Within

We can focus our expanding efforts with two questions: "Are we doing the right thing?" and "Are we doing it right?"

- To answer the question "Are we doing the right thing?" we focus upon **expanding beyond** to re-examine the reasons for our story, the contextual requirements upon our systems, or the conditions within which our 3D model is nested. If we discover information that shows us that the context, conditions, or reasons for what we have been doing up to this point have changed or are not accurate, then we might determine that we have been doing the "wrong thing."

- To answer the question "Are we doing it right?" we focus upon measuring the quality of the results, outputs, or functions we are thinking about. We may then examine the quality of the transformational processes or the resource inputs involved. In short, we may expand our thinking by **expanding within** our current operations to generate new operations.

The skill of expanding involves looking beyond our current reasons for what we are doing to generate a new direction, and looking within our current operations to generate new operations.

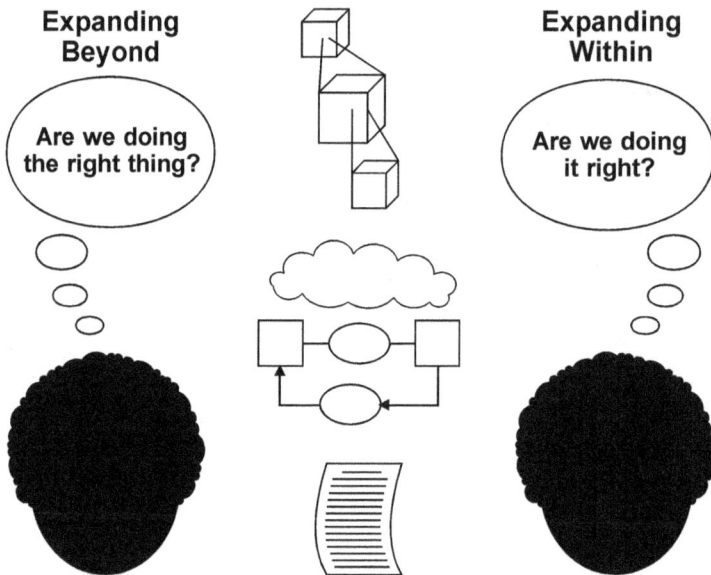

Expanding Beyond

When we "expand beyond" our current thinking, we gain perspective on our current operations by viewing them from at least one level higher: systems provide perspective for sentences; schematics provide perspective for systems. "Expanding beyond" means we ask ourselves how our current document, report, or letter (sentences) contributes to accomplishing our goals by viewing it against a "bigger picture" of what we are trying to accomplish (a systems representation, for example). Or, we might ask ourselves or others how our current system (systems diagram) contributes to accomplishing our goals as represented by our scales, matrices, or 3-D Models (schematics).

By "expanding beyond," we can gain a better perspective of the effectiveness of what we are doing. When we "expand beyond" our current thinking, we look a "level higher." Then, we can better see if we are "doing the right thing."

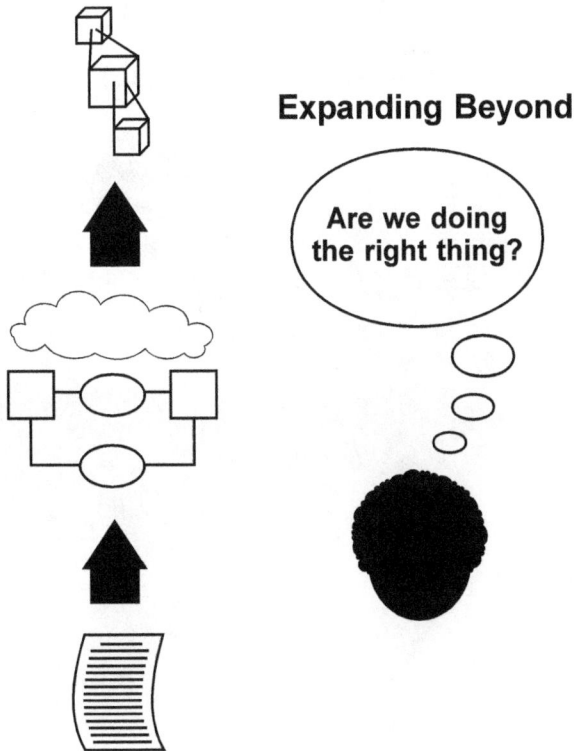

Expanding Beyond

Are we doing the right thing?

Expanding Within

When we "expand within" our current thinking, we look at the ingredients within our own sentences, systems, or schematics by expanding alternatives within our current information representations. We can expand any of the ingredients of our sentences, systems, or schematics. When we "expand within" by expanding alternatives we are asking ourselves "Are we doing things right?"

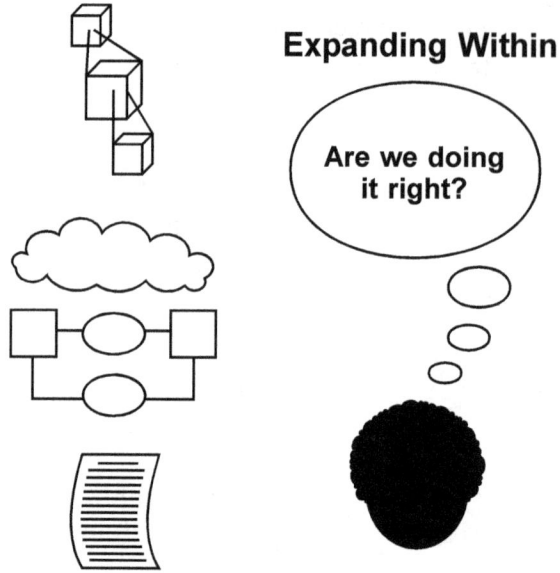

Expanding Within

Are we doing it right?

Summarizing Exploring—Goal-Setting, Analyzing, and Expanding

Exploring means setting goals, analyzing information, and expanding to generate new information.

Goal-setting begins with our own values as expressed by our interests. We may start with a specific reason or goal for wanting to think about particular information. Our goals will often change as we interact with new information. At some point, we will also experience pressures from outside ourselves upon the goals we are setting. We experience the expectations of others, project require-ments, time limitations, and many other external requirements. Setting goals involves negotiating these external requirements with our internal values.

When we analyze information, we break it into parts. We use the tools of representing—sentences, systems, or schematics—as a way to frame or build our analyses. By analyzing, we find out what we do know and discover some direction for learning or generating what we do not yet know.

Expanding requires that we innovate or generate to envision new possibili-ties and options. We may generate by "expanding beyond" because we are not certain that we have been "doing the right thing." We may generate by "expand-ing within" because we believe we are not "doing it right."

When we have completed our "exploring phase" of reasoning, we have made an analysis of the current operations of this problem or opportunity that is important to us. We have decided on a goal—our relationship with this problem or opportunity. Then, we have generated a new image of "the possible."

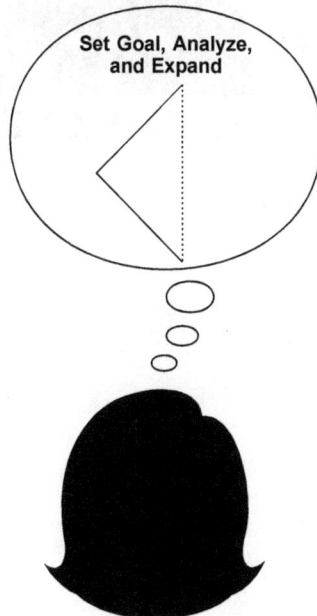

Set Goal, Analyze, and Expand

The Benefits of Exploring

Exploring to generate new information is a journey. We begin our intellectual journey by setting a goal. *Our goal is our reason for thinking.* We continue exploring when we analyze the current situation at a deeper level. *Our analysis is a record of our initial exploration.* We then use our analysis, this initial map, to stimulate our generativity. We systematically expand and explore new options "within" our initial map and/or "beyond" its borders. We are generative explorers, creating new possibilities.

With a map of new "possibilities" for our consideration, we will enter the next phase of reasoning—understanding.

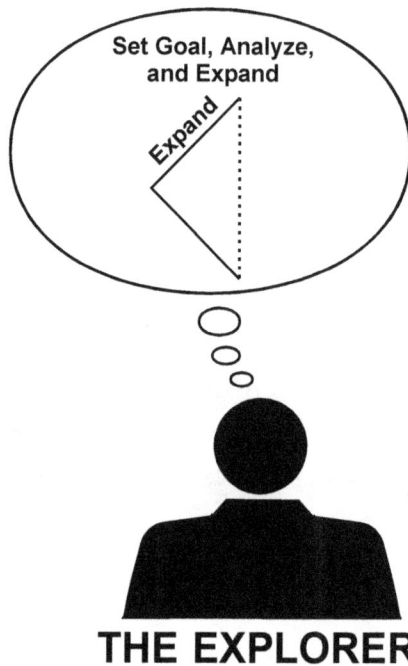

Set Goal, Analyze, and Expand

Expand

THE EXPLORER

Understanding by Narrowing

To explore information, we expand it to generate new options. Now, to understand information, we narrow it to select those parts that best satisfy our goals. We narrow to generate new information by bringing separate parts together into a whole. We narrow or select to change certain parts of our story by considering how each alternative sentence will impact our whole story and help us reach our goals. We narrow or select to change certain parts of our system by considering how well each new ingredient to our system will interact with the other parts to help us reach our goals. We narrow or select to change certain parts of our schematic representation by considering the effects of the interactions of the new dimensions upon the other dimensions to help us reach our goals.

In narrowing, we will select new combinations and permutations of ingredients resulting in new sentences, systems, and schematics. But how will we decide which changes are best?

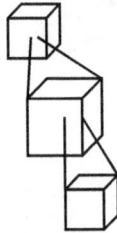

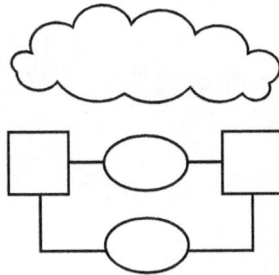

Narrowing by Deciding to Satisfy Goals

We narrow to select new sentences, system ingredients, or dimensions for our schematics by selecting those that best satisfy our goals. Realizing that our goals may have changed as we learned more about what is possible, we will revisit our internal values and the external requirements upon us to refine or redefine our goals.

Which sentence, system, or schematic ingredients can best satisfy both requirements and values? We will use decision-making strategies to determine how to best satisfy our goals.

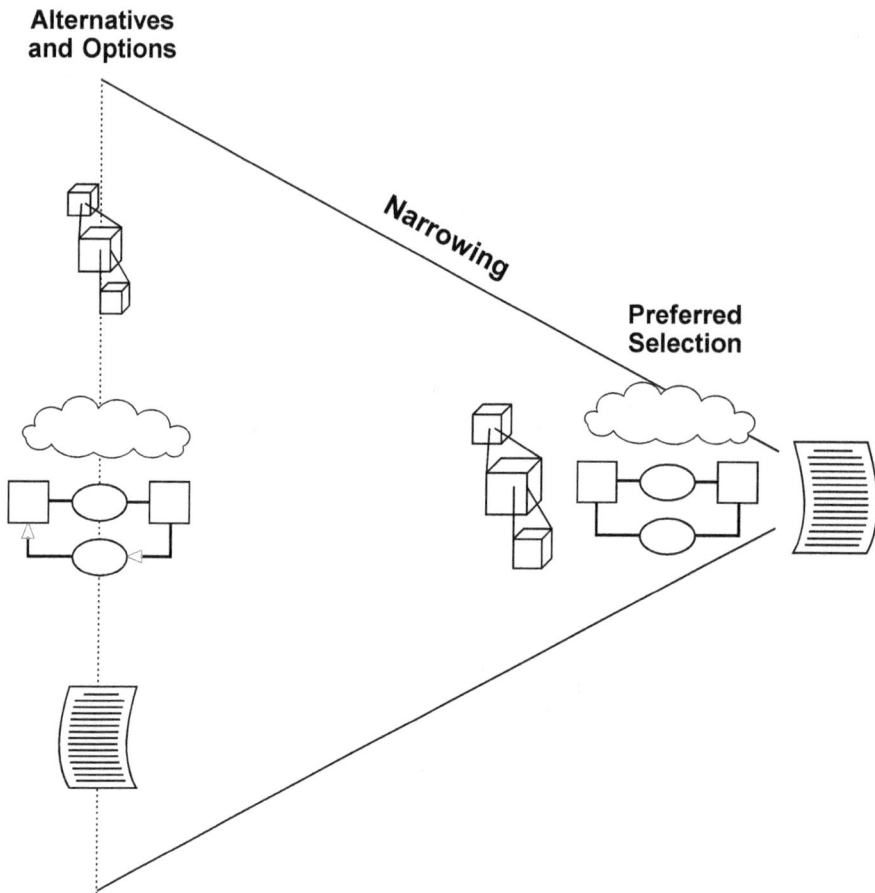

Deciding by Decision Making

We narrow or synthesize new information by making choices about which answers to our 5W2H questions, modifications of our system ingredients, or changes to the dimensions of our schematics we wish to make.

Decision making involves four steps:

1. Refer to your goals to help you **define** criteria or reasons for making your choices.

2. **Weigh** these criteria by deciding which ones are most important. (Rate them with a number value for each criterion. Use a number system, for example, with a 10 for most important.)

3. **List** your alternatives or choices.

4. **Calculate** which alternatives will best satisfy your criteria. (If an alternative rates high in satisfying a criterion, for example, rate it a +2. If it will be harmful to your criterion, rate it a -2. If a criterion will not be affected, rate the alternative a zero. **Multiply** the criterion weight by your rating of how well or poorly you predict each alternative will be satisfied by each criterion. Now add up your ratings and see what your decision-making chart tells you.)

When we make decisions, we may not always choose to draw a matrix and follow steps 1 through 4 as described. Many decisions will be easy to make because we have been focused on the choices—the alternatives, the criteria for making a choice—and know which criteria are most important. Other, more difficult choices can benefit from this four-step decision-making process. What is essential to remember about all decision making is to make choices with specific criteria or reasons in mind.

Understanding by narrowing means making choices about the new information we are generating.

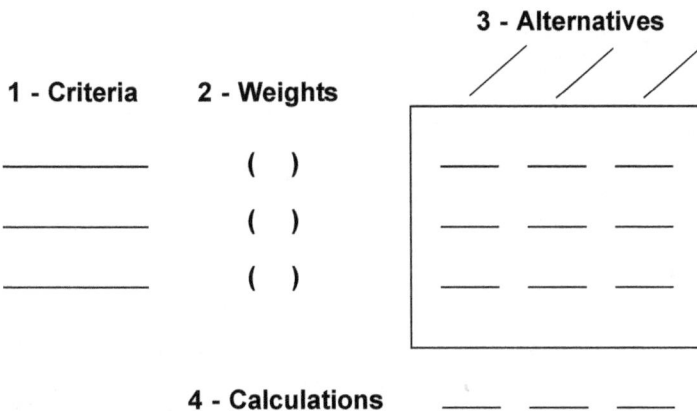

3 - Alternatives

1 - Criteria   **2 - Weights**

————————   ( )   — — —

————————   ( )   — — —

————————   ( )   — — —

4 - Calculations   — — —

Summarizing Understanding—Narrowing

Understanding means narrowing to generate new information. Expanding requires that we look beyond what we initially see to envision possibilities. We use the tools for building and representing information: sentences, systems, and schematics. Narrowing is a systematic process for synthesizing or "putting together" new information. When we complete our "understanding phase" of reasoning, we will create new information and new hypotheses to test.

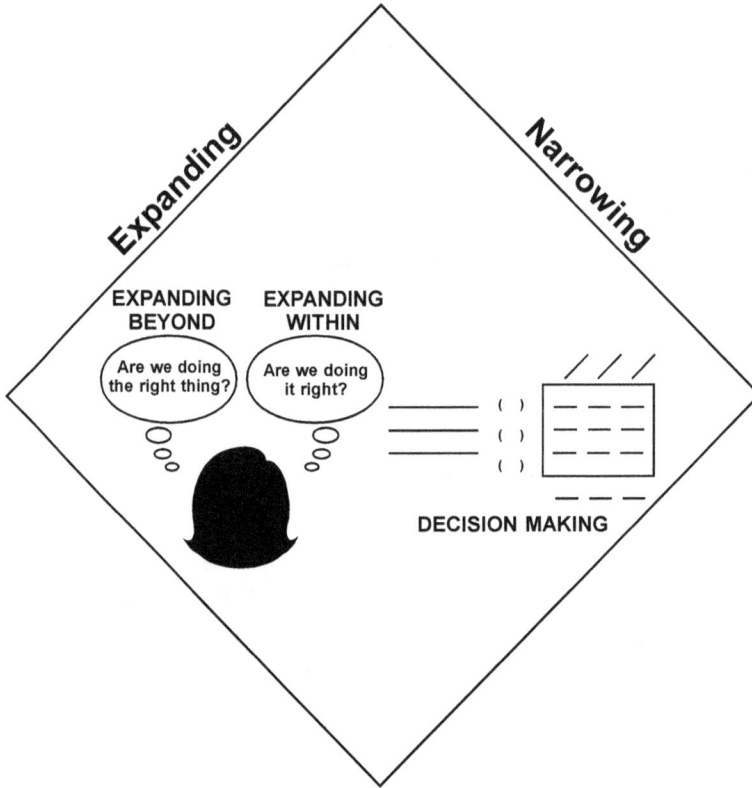

The Benefits of Understanding

We are all capable of creativity and generativity. The human mind is so wondrous, and life's problems and opportunities so stimulating, that we can almost not help but be creative. It is up to us to determine how we will use our brainpower. With skills for expanding and narrowing, we focus our creative energies and unleash the innovation within each of us.

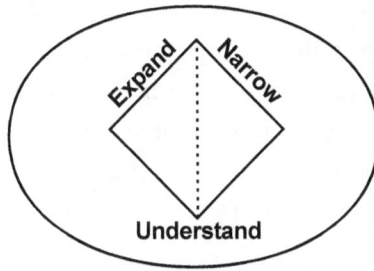

THE INNOVATOR

Acting—Planning, Performing, and Evaluating

When we set our goal and analyzed information related to it, we determined our reason for exploring and defined our starting point. When we expanded options and alternatives, we systematically generated a vision of what might be possible. When we systematically narrowed to decide on the best choices, we created our understanding of what we believed the information could become. Now, in acting, we give life to these possibilities by trying them out. Acting means transforming information into behavior. Acting involves *before, during* and *after* steps. Acting means *planning, performing,* and *evaluating.* We **plan** before we perform to maximize our chances for success. We **perform** to test our new hypotheses. We **evaluate** after our performance to maximize our learning and reinforce our successes.

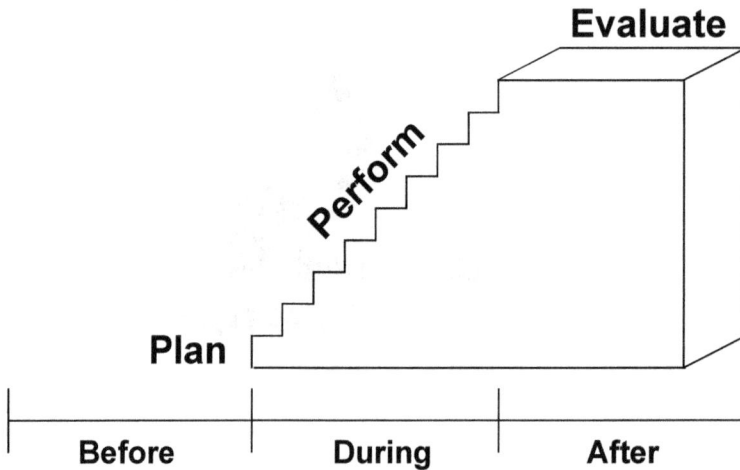

Acting by Planning

Planning means making a program for accomplishing something. We know what we want to accomplish because we expended the time and energy to relate with others and information. We represented this information and then explored and understood to create our own new ideas and information. Now, planning is about designing a program—a series of actions or activities—for bringing our ideas to life.

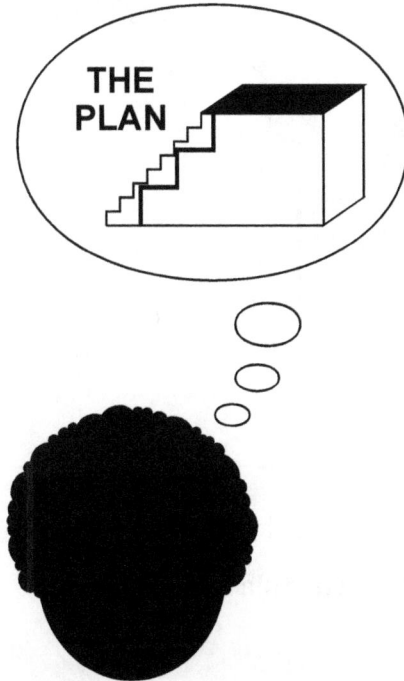

Planning

When we plan, we organize our goals—what we intend to do—into pieces that are of a size or magnitude that we can accomplish. Smaller goals are our objectives. We further divide these objectives into tasks and steps, and then fill in whatever sub-steps we think we need to include. Next, we add a timeline or a schedule. Our plan is now ready.

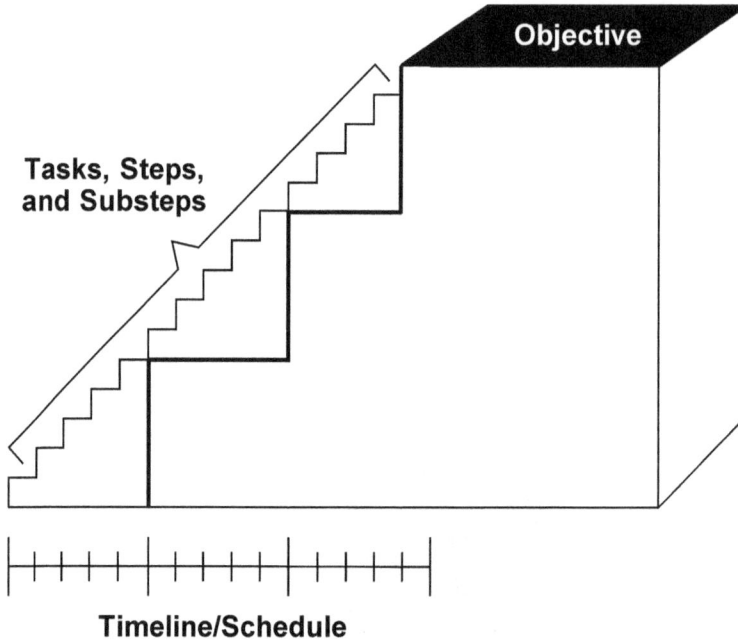

Objective

**Tasks, Steps,
and Substeps**

Timeline/Schedule

Acting by Performing

We have been relating, representing, and reasoning with others and with information. Now all our hard work and thinking come to life in our performance. We are confident and ready because we have used our brainpower to get us to this point. We are excited because we get to test out our hypotheses.

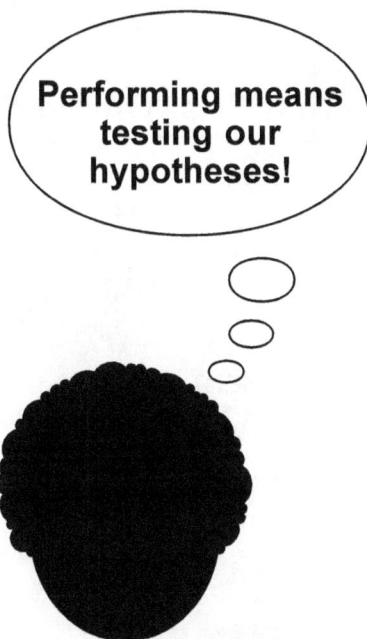

Performing means testing our hypotheses!

Performing

Performing means focusing our energies to accomplish our intentions. When we are performing, we become acutely sensitive as to when to slow down our pulse rates to focus still more intensely, or when to increase our adrenaline to help us access our memory files. Performing is an exciting time. All of the skills of "The New 3Rs" become available to us as we relate, represent, and reason "on-the-spot."

The New 3Rs "On-the-Spot"

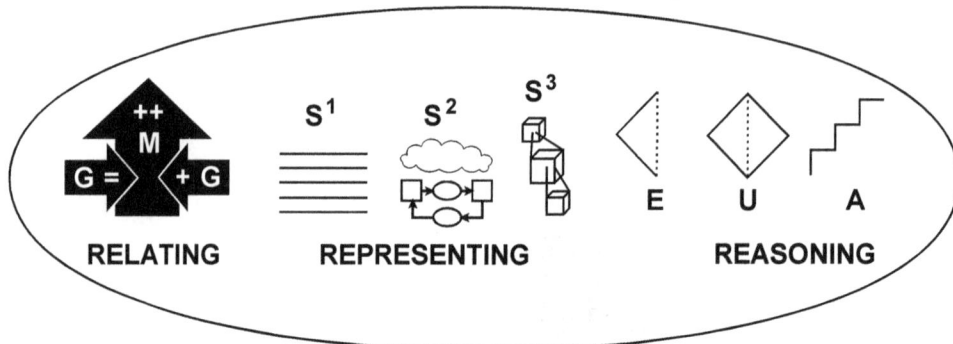

Hypothesis Testing by Evaluating

When we evaluate our performance, we compare our results with our goals. How well did we satisfy our values? How well did we satisfy requirements? How close did we come to satisfying both values and requirements?

Three common measures of performance are quantity, quality and timeliness:

- **Quantitative measures** tell us "how many" were completed or "how much" was accomplished.

- **Qualitative measures** tell us "how well" it was accomplished.

- **Timeliness measures** tell us whether the performance was "on time," "early," or "late."

We can use the answers to these questions as a source of our learning and our reinforcement.

Maximizing Values and Requirements

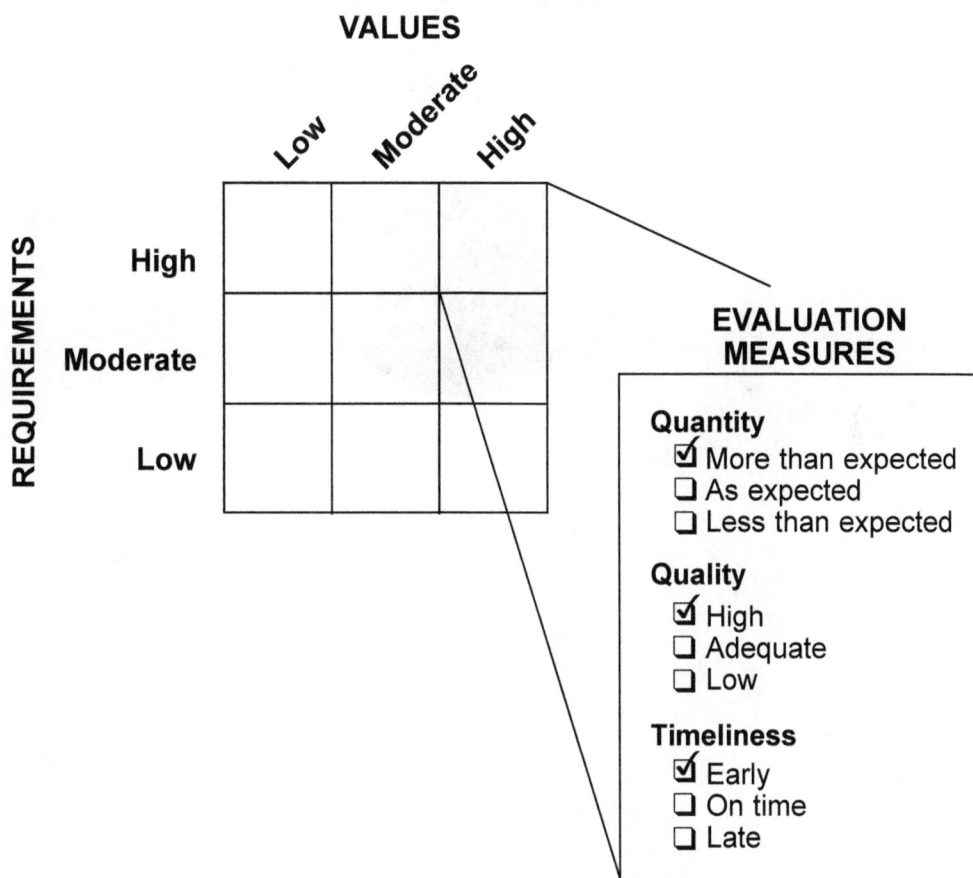

VALUES

Low   Moderate   High

REQUIREMENTS

High
Moderate
Low

EVALUATION MEASURES

Quantity
☑ More than expected
❑ As expected
❑ Less than expected

Quality
☑ High
❑ Adequate
❑ Low

Timeliness
☑ Early
❑ On time
❑ Late

Evaluating

When we evaluate, we appraise our performance. Evaluation is essential for both **learning** and **reinforcement.** Some of what we do may disappoint us. We can find out what we might have done better or differently. This is the source of our learning. Some of what we do will make us satisfied that we expended our energy on this work. We need to acknowledge our satisfaction. We need to take a moment and enjoy our feelings of accomplishment. We need to reinforce ourselves because reinforcement may not come to us from others. When we reinforce ourselves we associate our hard work with a good feeling and remember the positive aspects of our performance. Reinforcement is essential if we intend to work hard on another occasion. We evaluate for both learning and reinforcement reasons.

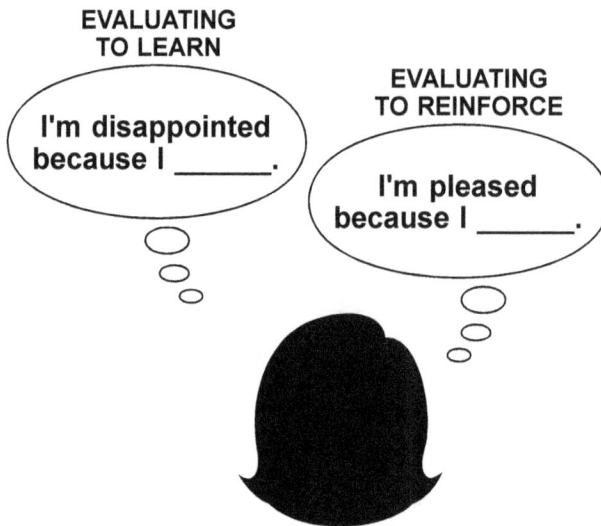

Evaluating to Learn

Every crisis is an opportunity to grow. When we dare to create hypotheses and test them, we put ourselves at risk. The difference between a creative person, and one who is not, begins with a willingness to take a risk. Without risk, no creativity is possible. With a willingness to risk and a skilled approach to thinking (like The New 3Rs), a world of possibilities opens up for us.

Sometimes, risks result in failure. Failure delivers too: it brings us learning. When we evaluate to find out what went wrong, we learn and grow.

Evaluating to Reinforce

Success results in benefits for which we can be justly pleased. When our evaluations show us our successes, it is important that we celebrate. There are many ways to celebrate. We can determine how to reinforce ourselves or others by considering the reinforcers that move us. We may reinforce ourselves or others with a gathering or party. Maybe an award or a financial "bonus" is appropriate. Maybe some time off would be appropriate. A run in the park? A hike in the woods? For creative people, the greatest reinforcer is "another opportunity to create and test a hypothesis—another chance to think!"

Summarizing Acting—Hypothesis Testing by Planning, Performing, and Evaluating

Acting means transforming information into behavior. When we act, we try out our new information. We act by planning, performing, and evaluating. When we plan, we organize our performance into pieces we can accomplish. We plan by dividing our efforts into objectives, tasks, steps, and sub-steps. We also define a timeline or schedule. We apply The New 3Rs "on-the-spot" as we perform. We use the skills of relating, representing, and reasoning as we need them. Evaluation means measuring the quantity, quality, and timeliness of our performance so we can learn from it and reinforce our efforts. Acting means planning, performing, and evaluating.

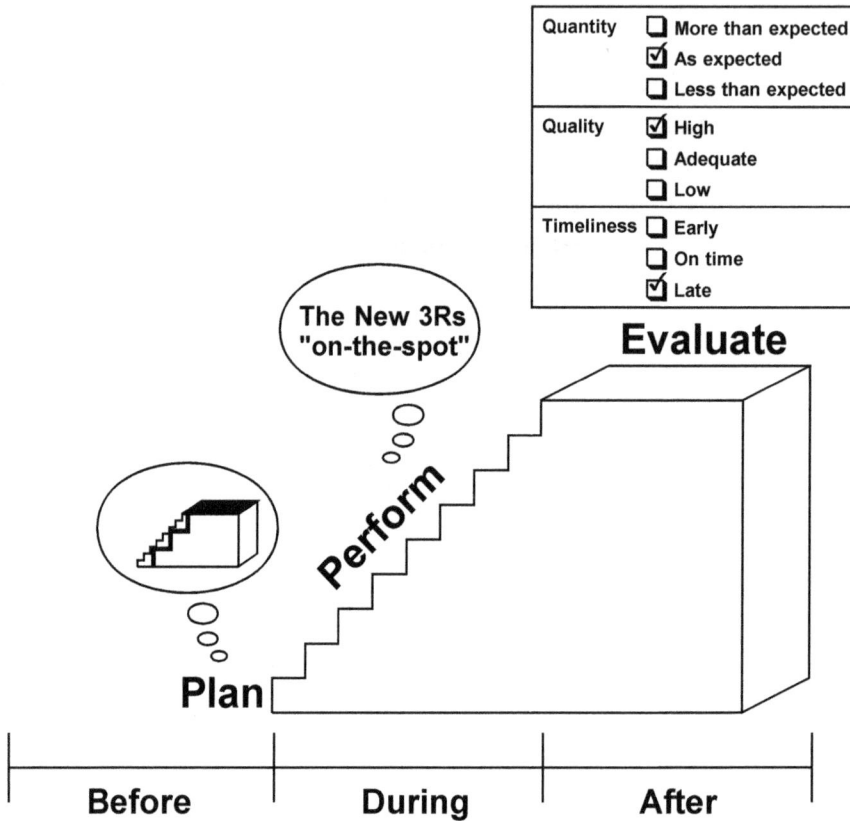

Quantity	☐ More than expected
	☑ As expected
	☐ Less than expected
Quality	☑ High
	☐ Adequate
	☐ Low
Timeliness	☐ Early
	☐ On time
	☑ Late

The New 3Rs "on-the-spot"

Evaluate

Perform

Plan

Before | During | After

112

The Benefits of Acting

We are all hypothesis-testers when we decide we want to be. If we never try, we'll never know what is possible. When we act, we are running an experiment. We are finding out what works and what does not. With skills for acting we are not overwhelmed by the thought of trying out something new. If we want to, we can do it. And, we will reap all the possible learning and potential rewards that action begets.

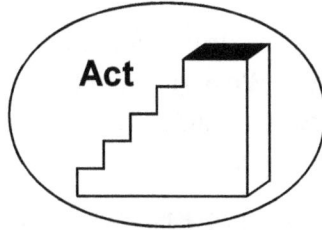

THE HYPOTHESIS TESTER

Summarizing Reasoning

We reason by exploring, understanding, and acting upon information.

- **Exploring**—When we *explore,* we conceive of new possibilities for the original information. We can all become more effective investigators.

- **Understanding**—When we are in the *understanding* phase of reasoning, we narrow or select what we believe to be the best of the new information we have generated. We can all become more innovative and creative.

- **Acting**—When we *act* upon our new ideas we bring them to life. We develop a plan for success. We perform to transform the plan into behavior. We evaluate to learn and reinforce future actions. We can all become disciplined hypothesis testers.

We learn to improve our reasoning processes when we show and tell our skills for reasoning. Reasoning together means exploring, understanding, and acting together.

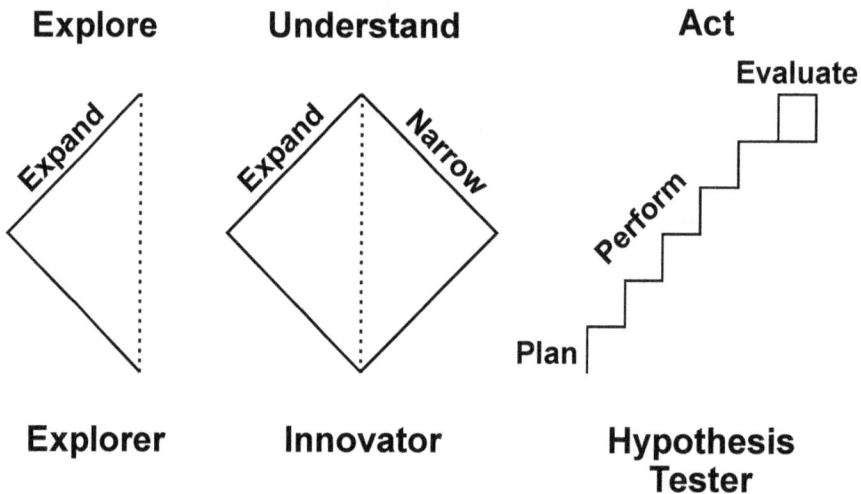

III

Summary

6

The Possibilities Person

The New 3Rs

We now live in an age of unprecedented access to new and growing sources of information. The 3Rs of reading, 'riting and 'rithmetic remain basic skills that we all need. Yet, reading, writing, and math are no longer an adequate skill set for our time. The New 3Rs help us handle the requirements and opportunities of our growing and changing information environment.

The New 3Rs skills are easy to remember: Relating, Representing and Reasoning. Relating means getting, giving, and merging (GGM). Representing means using sentences, systems, and schematics (The 3Ss). Reasoning means exploring, understanding and acting (EUA). These are the skills that we all need to conquer and harness to be empowered to full participation in our information environment.

These are the skills we need to generate new ideas—to think freely and live free.

The New 3Rs

RELATING	REPRESENTING	REASONING
Merge	Schematics	Act
Give	Systems	Understand
Get	Sentences	Explore

Relating Skills—GGM: Get, Give, Merge

Relating can be thought of as getting, giving, and merging with people and all other sources of information. How skillfully do we relate?

- Are we empathic with people and other sources of information? In other words, are we using all the skills we need to get the messages that are being presented to us?

- Are we additive with people and other sources of information? Another way of asking this: are we using the best methods to give information to others?

- Are we inclusive with people and other sources of information? In other words, are we actively convincing, conceding, negotiating or generating to **merge** ideas and directions?

Relating means being empathic, additive, and inclusive. Relating is accomplished by getting, giving, and merging.

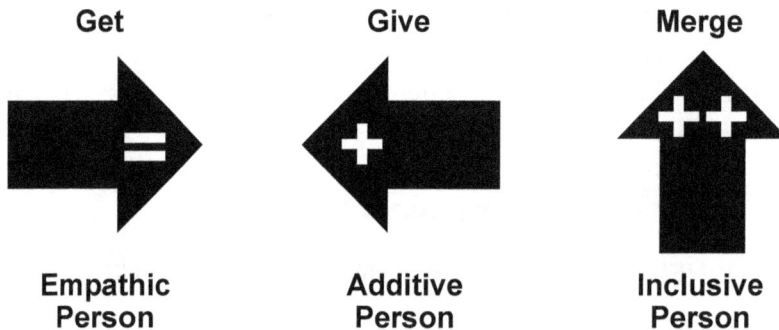

Get	Give	Merge
=	+	++
Empathic Person	**Additive Person**	**Inclusive Person**

Representing Skills—The 3Ss:
Sentences, Systems, Schematics

Being skilled in representing information can be described as being facile with sentences, systems and schematics. How skillfully do we represent information?

- Are we articulate in the formulation and presentation of our verbal and written messages? In other words, are our **sentences** well formulated and comprehensive in answering the 5W2H questions?

- Do our messages communicate a **systems** perspective of the information we are presenting? Another way of asking this: are we showing systems representations of information to others?

- Are we modeling information to present its various dimensions? In other words are we presenting information in **schematics**: 1D scales, 2D matrices and 3D models?

Representing means formulating and presenting accurate and communicative verbal and written messages, systems perspectives, and schematic models. Representing is accomplished with sentences, systems, and schematics.

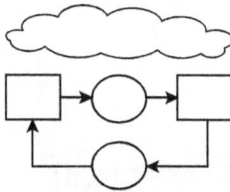

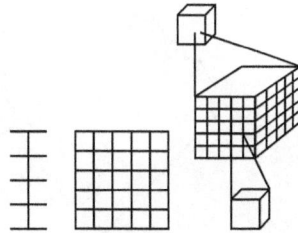

Sentences	Systems	Schematics
Articulate Reporter	**Systems Scientist**	**Information Modeler**

Reasoning Skills—EUA: Explore, Understand, Act

We can explain our reasoning processes as exploring, understanding, and acting upon information. How skillfully do we reason and model our reasoning processes?

- Are we generative explorers? In other words, do we systematically **explore** by setting goals, analyzing information, and expanding to generate new options and alternatives—new possibilities?

- Are we creative and innovative? Another way of asking this is: do we systematically **understand** by narrowing to generate specific new insights and new information that can be acted upon?

- Are we hypothesis testers? In other words, do we systematically **act** by planning, performing, and evaluating the products we make and the services we provide?

Reasoning means being an explorer, an innovator, and a hypothesis tester. Reasoning is accomplished by exploring, understanding, and acting.

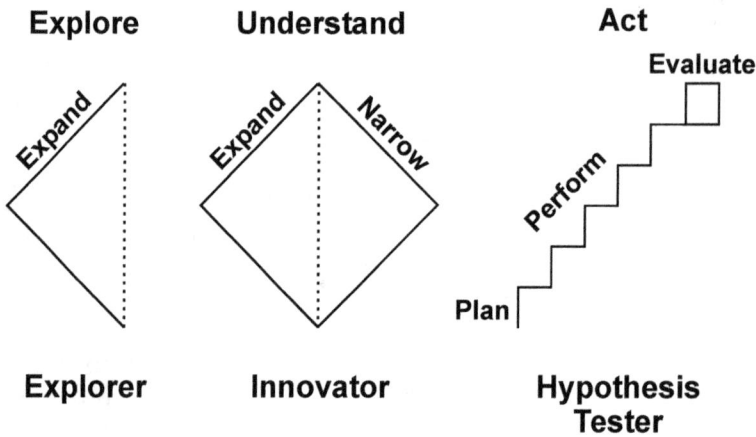

Explore   **Understand**   **Act**

Evaluate

Expand   Expand   Narrow

Perform

Plan

Explorer   **Innovator**   **Hypothesis Tester**

The New 3Rs: Possibilities Thinking and Individual Freedom

When we use The New 3Rs to relate, represent and reason, we become "Possibilities People." When we skillfully and intentionally use the skills of The New 3Rs, we free ourselves and others to the possibilities of new ideas and the development of new information.

The New 3Rs are skills for freedom. We no longer need to accept the shackles of our conditioned habits. We can find increased freedom when we learn and apply the best solutions that others have created. And, with The New 3Rs, we are empowered with skills to innovate and generate—to actualize our individual freedom.

It is up to each of us to apply what we know about The New 3Rs—Relating, Representing, and Reasoning: Skills for possibilities thinking and individual freedom. Imagine the possibilities!

Appendix

GET by ATTENDING

- **Prepare**
- **Square and lean**
- **Make eye contact**

Attending to Others

Attending to Information

ATTENDING

EMPATHIC PERSON

From *The New 3Rs: Relating, Representing, and Reasoning*
© 2013 by Carkhuff Thinking Systems, Inc.

GET by OBSERVING

- Observe appearance
- Observe behaviors
- Consider inferences

Observing Others

Observing Information

OBSERVING

EMPATHIC PERSON

GET by LISTENING

- **Resist distractions**

- **Listen for specifics**

- **Discover the theme**

Listening to Others

Listening to Information

LISTENING

EMPATHIC PERSON

GET by RESPONDING

3. Interchangeable Meaning

You're __(feeling)__ because __(reason)__ .

2. Interchangeable Feeling

You're __(feeling)__ .

1. Interchangeable Content

You're saying __(content)__ .

RESPONDING

EMPATHIC PERSON

From *The New 3Rs: Relating, Representing, and Reasoning*
© 2013 by Carkhuff Thinking Systems, Inc.

GIVE

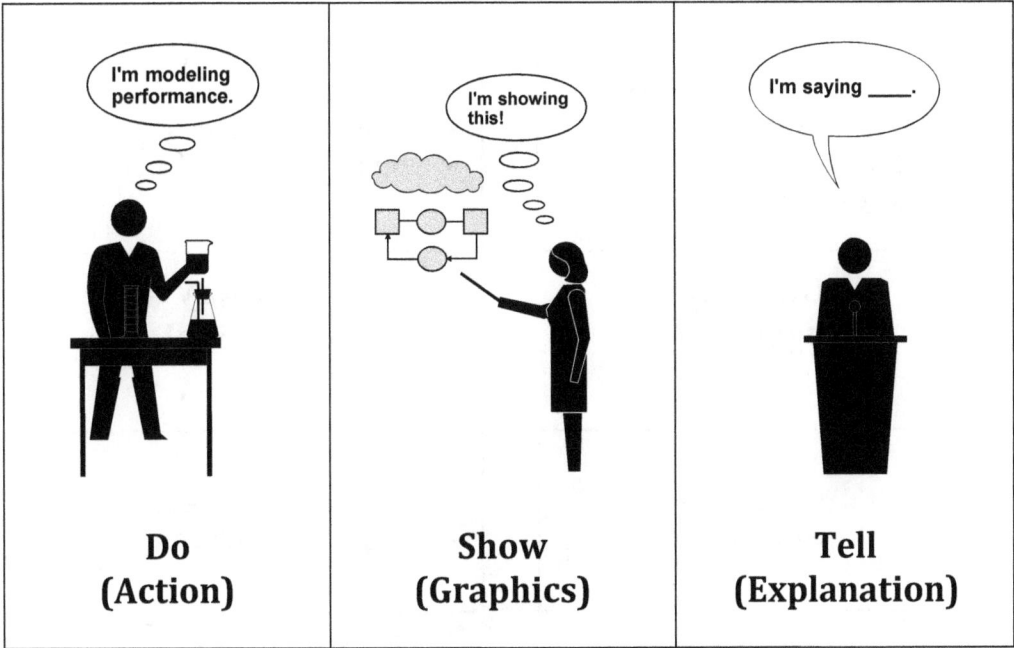

| Do
(Action) | Show
(Graphics) | Tell
(Explanation) |

ADDITIVE PERSON

MERGE

• Acknowledge agreement • Negotiate differences • Summarize negotiated agreement	• Mutual exploration • Mutual understanding • Mutual action
Our Way (Negotiating)	**A New Way (Generating)**
Improve your presentation.	Accept the other person's position.
My Way (Convincing)	**Your Way (Conceding)**

INCLUSIVE PERSON

From *The New 3Rs: Relating, Representing, and Reasoning*
© 2013 by Carkhuff Thinking Systems, Inc.

S¹ – SENTENCES

When __who & what__ ,
by __how & why__ ,
then __what__ ,
so that __when, where & why__ ,
as measured by __how well__ .

The Language of Sentences	Communicating with Sentences
(5W2H)	• Objectives (measurements)
• Who	• Applications (uses)
• What	• Principles (explanations)
• When	• Concepts (relationships)
• Where	• Facts (labels)
• Why	
• How	
• How Well	

ARTICULATE REPORTER

From *The New 3Rs: Relating, Representing, and Reasoning*
© 2013 by Carkhuff Thinking Systems, Inc.

S² – SYSTEMS

**CONDITIONS/
CONTEXT**

When, Where, Why

RESOURCE INPUTS	PROCESSES	RESULTS OUTPUTS
Who What	How Why	What

**FEEDBACK
METRICS**

How
Well

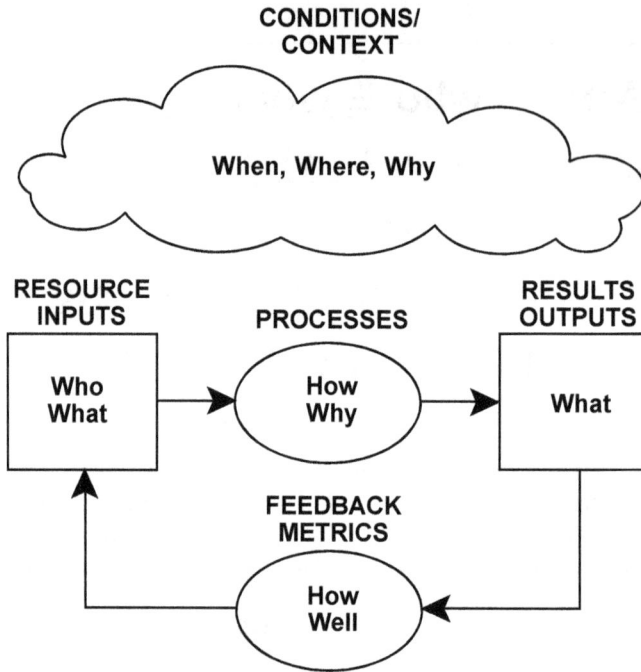

The Language of Systems	Communicating with Systems
• Outputs • Inputs • Processes • Context • Feedback	• Results • Resources • Processes • Conditions • Metrics

SYSTEMS SCIENTIST

From The New 3Rs: Relating, Representing, and Reasoning
© 2013 by Carkhuff Thinking Systems, Inc.

132

S³ – SCHEMATICS

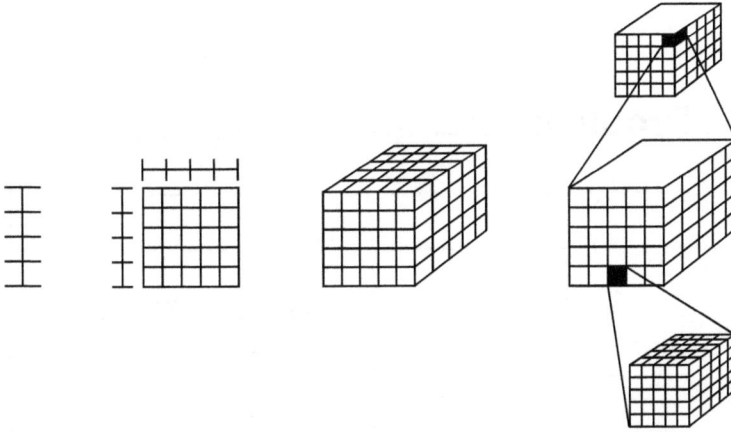

The Language of Schematics	Communicating with Schematics
• Functions • Components • Processes • Conditions • Standards	• Multi-Nested 3D Model • Nested 3D Model • 3D Model • 2D Matrix • 1D Scale

INFORMATION MODELER

From *The New 3Rs: Relating, Representing, and Reasoning*
© 2013 by Carkhuff Thinking Systems, Inc.

EXPLORE

Goal-Setting

Problem or Opportunity _____
_____

Values	Requirements
⊢ _____	⊢ _____
⊢ _____	⊢ _____
⊢ _____	⊢ _____

Explorer

EXPLORE

Analyzing

Goal-Setting and Analyzing with Schematics

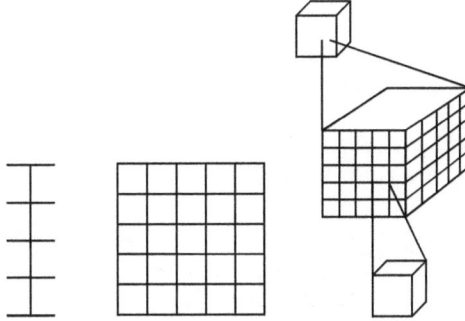

Goal-Setting and Analyzing with Systems

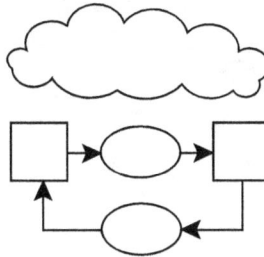

Goal-Setting and Analyzing with Sentences

Explorer

EXPLORE

Expanding

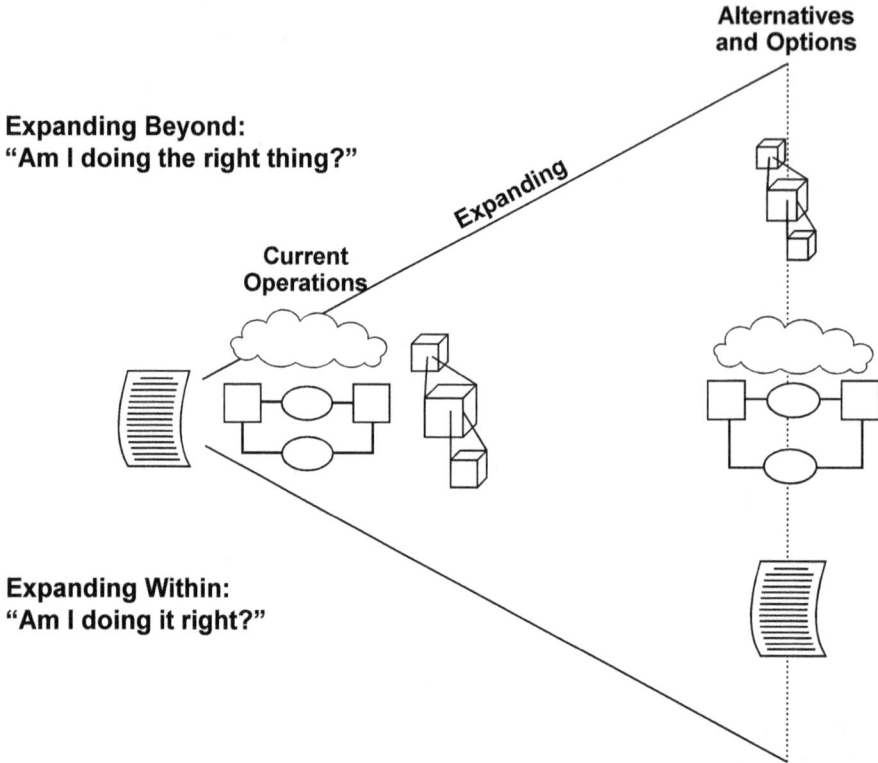

**Alternatives
and Options**

**Expanding Beyond:
"Am I doing the right thing?"**

Expanding

**Current
Operations**

**Expanding Within:
"Am I doing it right?"**

Explorer

From *The New 3Rs: Relating, Representing, and Reasoning*
© 2013 by Carkhuff Thinking Systems, Inc.

UNDERSTAND

Narrowing

**Alternatives
and Options**

Expanding   *Narrowing*

**Current
Operations**

**Preferred
Selection**

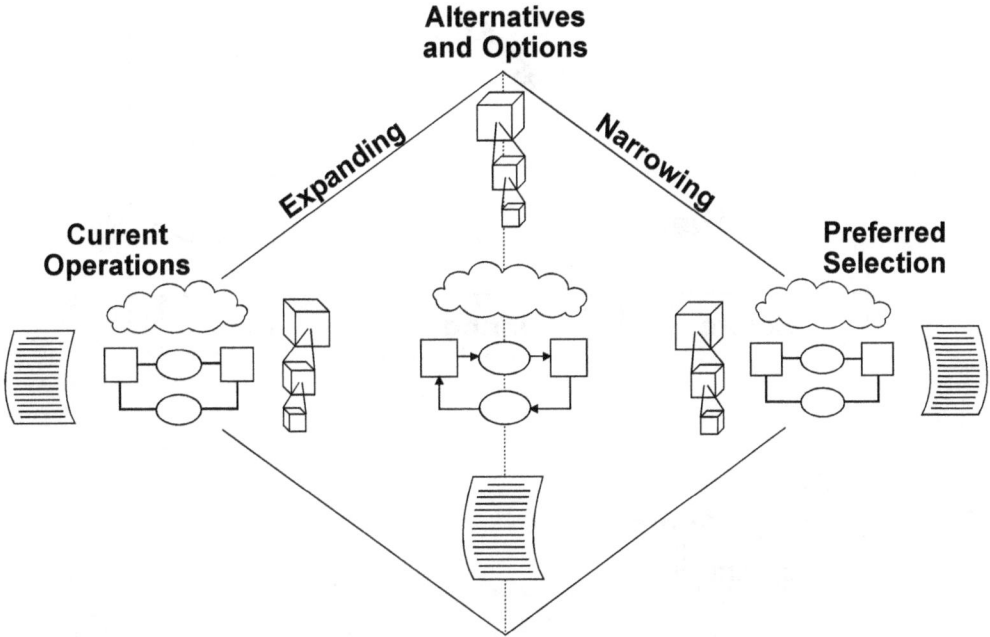

Decision Making

1. Criteria
2. Weights
3. Alternatives
4. Calculations

Innovator

From *The New 3Rs: Relating, Representing, and Reasoning*
© 2013 by Carkhuff Thinking Systems, Inc.

ACT

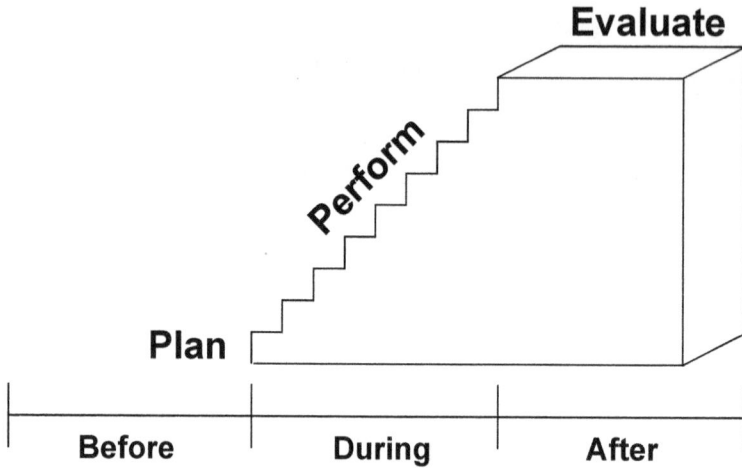

1. Plan

   - Objectives
   - Tasks, Steps, Substeps
   - Timeline/Schedule

2. Perform
   "On-the-Spot New 3Rs"

3. Evaluate
   - Evaluate to Learn from What Did Not Work
   - Evaluate to Reinforce What Worked

Hypothesis Tester

From The New 3Rs: Relating, Representing, and Reasoning
© 2013 by Carkhuff Thinking Systems, Inc.

References

Anthony, W. *The Principles of Psychiatric Rehabilitation.* Baltimore, MD: University Park Press, 1979.

Aspy, D. N., and Roebuck, F. N. *Kids Don't Learn from People They Don't Like.* Amherst, MA: HRD Press, 1977.

Banks, G. *From Bondage through Prosperity: Finding the Freedom in Thinking.* Amherst, MA: HRD Press, 2013.

Berenson, B. G. *The Possibilities Mind.* Amherst, MA: HRD Press, 2001.

Berenson, B. G. *Carkhuff and The Human Sciences.* McLean, VA: The McLean Project, 2013.

Berenson, B. G. and Cannon, J. R. *The Science of Freedom.* Amherst, MA: HRD Press, 2006.

Berners-Lee, T. *Weaving the Web.* Britain: Orion Business, 1989, ISBN 0-7528-2090-7.

Bierman, R. *Toward Meeting Fundamental Human Service Needs.* Guelph, Ontario: Human Service Community, Inc., 1976.

Bugelski, B. R. *Psychology of Learning.* New York: Holt, Rinehart & Winston, 1956.

Bugelski, B. R. *Principles of Learning.* New York: Praeger, 1979.

Carkhuff, R. R. *Helping and Human Relations. Volumes I and II.* New York: Holt, Rinehart & Winston, 1969.

Carkhuff, R. R. *The Development of Human Resources.* New York: Holt, Rinehart & Winston, 1971.

Carkhuff, R. R. *The Promise of America.* Amherst, MA: HRD Press, 1974.

Carkhuff, R. R. *Toward Actualizing Human Potential.* Amherst, MA: HRD Press, 1981.

Carkhuff, R. R. *Sources of Human Productivity.* Amherst, MA: HRD Press, 1983.

Carkhuff, R. R. *The Exemplar.* Amherst, MA: HRD Press, 1984.

Carkhuff, R. R. *Human Processing and Human Productivity.* Amherst, MA: HRD Press, 1986.

Carkhuff, R. R. *The Age of the New Capitalism.* Amherst, MA: HRD Press, 1988.

Carkhuff, R. R. *Empowering.* Amherst, MA: HRD Press, 1989.

Carkhuff, R. R. *Human Possibilities.* Amherst, MA: HRD Press, 2000.

Carkhuff, R. R. *The Age of Ideation.* Amherst, MA: HRD Press, 2007.

Carkhuff, R. R. *The Art of Helping.* Ninth Edition. Amherst, MA: HRD Press, 2009.

Carkhuff, R. R. *Saving America: The Generativity Solution.* Amherst, MA: HRD Press, 2010.

Carkhuff, R. R. *The Human Sciences: Volume I. Probabilities, Possibilities, and Generativity Sciences.* Amherst, MA: HRD Press, 2013.

Carkhuff, R. R. *The Human Sciences: Volume II. Probabilities, Possibilities, and Generativity Technologies.* Amherst, MA: HRD Press, 2013.

Carkhuff, R. R. *TheMcLeanProject.com.* The McLean Project, 2011.

Carkhuff, R. R. *Human Generativity: An Introduction to Human Sciences.* Amherst, MA: HRD Press, 2013.

Carkhuff, R. R. and Berenson, B. G. *The New Science of Possibilities. Volumes I and II.* Amherst, MA: HRD Press, 2000.

Carkhuff, R. R. and Berenson, B. G., et al. *The Possibilities Organization.* Amherst, MA: HRD Press, 2000.

Carkhuff, R. R. and Berenson, B. G., et al. *The Possibilities Leader.* Amherst, MA: HRD Press, 2000.

Carkhuff, R. R. and Berenson, B. G., et al. *Freedom-Building.* Amherst, MA: HRD Press, 2003.

Carkhuff, R. R. and Berenson, B. G., et al. *The Freedom Doctrine.* Amherst, MA: HRD Press, 2003.

Carkhuff, R. R. and Berenson, B. G., et al. *The Freedom Wars.* Amherst, MA: HRD Press, 2005.

Carkhuff, R. R. and Berenson, B. G., et al. *The Possibilities Economy.* Amherst, MA: HRD Press, 2006.

Drasgow, J. "Eclipsing All Great Works." Foreword, *The Freedom Wars.* Amherst, MA: HRD Press, 2000.

Einstein, A. *Relativity: The Special and General Theory.* New York: Henry Holt, 1931.

Einstein, A. *The Evolution of Physics.* Cambridge: University of Cambridge, 1938.

Einstein, A. *Collected Papers of Albert Einstein.* Princeton, NJ: Princeton University Press, 1989.

Hebb, D. O. *The Organization of Behavior.* New York: John Wiley and Sons, 1949.

Hull, C. L. *Mathematics—Deductive Theory of Rote Learning.* New York: Appleton–Century–Crofts, 1940.

Hull, C. L. *Principles of Behavior.* New York: Appleton–Century–Crofts, 1943.

Hull, C. L. *A Behavior System.* New Haven, CT: Yale University Press, 1952.

Kakovitch, T. *Collegium.* McLean, VA: The McLean Project, 2012.

Kakovitch, T. *The Fifth Force.* Amherst, MA: HRD Press, 2012.

Kilby, J. *First Successful Demonstration of Integrating a Transition with Resistors and Capacitors on a Simple Semiconductor Chip Defining the Monolithic Idea.* Dallas, TX: Texas Instruments, September 12, 1958.

Pavlov, I. P. *Conditioned Reflexes.* Oxford: Oxford University Press, 1927.

Rogers, C. R. "The Necessary and Sufficient Conditions of Therapeutic Personality Change." *Journal of Consulting Psychology,* 1957, 22, 95–103.

Siegel, S. *Nonparametric Statistics for the Behavioral Sciences.* Washington, DC: American Association for the Advancement of Science, 1959.

Sprinthall, R. C. *Basic Statistical Analysis.* Boston, MA: Allyn and Bacon, 2011.

Sprinthall, R. C. "Psychenomics." Afterword in R. R. Carkhuff, *Saving America: The Generativity Solution.* Amherst, MA: HRD Press, 2010.

Sprinthall, R. C. *SPSS.* Boston, MA: Pearson Education, Inc., 2009.

Straus, E. *Phenomenology: Pure and Applied.* Pittsburgh: Duquesne University Press, 1964.

Truax, C. B. and Carkhuff, R. R. *Toward Effective Counseling and Therapy.* Chicago: Aldine, 1967.

Watson, J. *Behaviorism.* Chicago: University of Chicago Press, 1930.

www.ingramcontent.com/pod-product-compliance
Lightning Source LLC
Chambersburg PA
CBHW081506200326
41518CB00015B/2399